Francisco Bruquetas & Michelle de la Calle

SPANISH FOR HEALTH CARE

USING ENGLISH TO LEARN SPANISH

SPANISH FOR HEALTH CARE
USING ENGLISH TO LEARN SPANISH
© 2012 Francisco and Michelle de la Calle

ISBN: 978-0-578-09812-8

R140427

Cover Art: Francisco de la Calle

Bruquetas Publishing
88 S. Third St. #162, San José, California 95112, USA
www.BruquetasPublishing.com

All rights reserved

No part of this book may be reproduced in any manner without permission in writing from Bruquetas Publishing.

For Katherine Lueder

The Book at a Glance

INTRODUCTION 14

SECTION I   SOUNDS
1.   THE ALPHABET 20
2.   THE VOWELS 26
3.   THE CONSONANTS 30
4.   ACCENT 40

SECTION II   WORDS
5.   SINGULAR / PLURAL 48
6.   MASCULINE / FEMININE 60
7.   CONJUGATION 68
8.   HOW TO LEARN WORDS EFFICIENTLY 80

SECTION III   SENTENCES
9.   ONE FUTURE, PRESENT, AND PAST 90
10. IRREGULARITIES IN FUTURE, PRESENT AND PAST ... 98
11. GRAMMAR RULES 106
12. NEGATIONS AND QUESTIONS 118

SECTION IV   VERBS

13. VERY IMPORTANT VERBS *124*
14. TRANSLATING "IT APPEALS TO ME" *134*
15. REFLEXIVITY AND PASSIVE VOICE *140*
16. THE PRESENT AND THE PAST TENSES *146*
17. NEXT STEPS IN SPANISH *154*

PHRASEBOOK *164*

APPENDICES

APPENDIX A: NOTES ABOUT DIALECTS *180*
APPENDIX B: NOTES ABOUT CULTURE *186*
APPENDIX C: PRESENT TENSE *194*
APPENDIX D: TABLE OF ENDINGS OF REGULAR VERBS.... *204*

INDEX OF GRAMMATICAL WORDS *208*

INDEX OF MEDICAL WORDS *216*

Table of Contents

INTRODUCTION 14

SECTION I   SOUNDS

1. THE ALPHABET 20
    - OTHER SYMBOLS 21
    - TIPS 21
    - GENERAL VOCABULARY 22
        - *The names of the letters in the alphabet* 22
    - MEDICAL VOCABULARY 23
        - *Samples of Spanish medical words that are similar in English* .. 23

2. THE VOWELS 26
    - TIPS 27
    - GENERAL VOCABULARY 28
        - *Numbers from 0 to 10* 28
    - MEDICAL VOCABULARY 29
        - *Systems* 29

3. THE CONSONANTS 30
    - RULES OF THUMB ON SPELLING 34
    - TIPS 35
    - GENERAL VOCABULARY 38
        - *Spanish-speaking Countries* 38
        - *Medical specialties* 39

4. ACCENT 40
    - RULE OF THUMB ON STRESS 41
    - TIPS 42
    - GENERAL VOCABULARY 43
        - *Interjections and greetings* 43
    - MEDICAL VOCABULARY 44
        - *Specialists* 44

SECTION II   WORDS

5. **SINGULAR / PLURAL** 48
   - **NUMBERS** 50
   - **TELLING THE TIME** 53
   - **TELLING THE DATE** 54
   - **TIPS** 54
   - **GENERAL VOCABULARY** 56
     - *Days of the week* 56
     - *Months of the year* 56
     - *Time units (in natural order)* 57
     - *Other words to express time* 57
     - *Location* 57
   - **MEDICAL VOCABULARY** 58
     - *Parts of the head* 58
     - *Quick reference of the external parts of the head* 59

6. **MASCULINE / FEMININE** 60
   - **BASIC RULES TO KNOW THE GENDER OF A WORD** 61
   - **GENERAL VOCABULARY** 63
     - *Articles and demonstratives (in natural order)* 63
     - *Possessives (in natural order)* 63
     - *Other limiting adjectives* 64
     - *The family* 65
     - *Genders and ages* 65
   - **MEDICAL VOCABULARY** 66
     - *Parts of the body* 66
     - *Quick reference of the external parts of the body* 67

7. **CONJUGATION** 68
   - **THE PERSONAL PRONOUNS** 71
   - **REGULAR VERBS** 73
   - **"TENER" (= TO HAVE)** 75
   - **TIPS** 75
   - **GENERAL VOCABULARY** 77
     - *Personal pronouns* 77
     - *The verbs for "to be" (= ser/ estar)* 77
     - *The verbs for "to have" (= tener/ haber)* 78
     - *Sample of descriptive adjectives that use "ser"* 78
     - *Sample of descriptive adjectives that use "estar"* 78
   - **MEDICAL VOCABULARY** 79
     - *Organs* 79

8. **HOW TO LEARN WORDS EFFICIENTLY** 80
   - COGNATES, INDIRECT COGNATES AND FALSE COGNATES 81
   - SPANGLISH 83
   - PREFIXES AND SUFFIXES 84
   - TIPS 84
   - GENERAL VOCABULARY 85
     - *Remember "tener" (to have got)* 85
     - *The verb "hacer" (= to make)* 85
     - *Nouns that go with "tener" (= to have got)* 85
     - *Nouns that go with "hacer" (= to make)* 86
     - *Spanglish* 86
   - MEDICAL VOCABULARY 87
     - *Bones* 87

SECTION III SENTENCES

9. **ONE FUTURE, PRESENT, AND PAST** 90
   - ONE FUTURE: "I AM GOING TO SING" 91
   - ONE PRESENT "I AM SINGING" 92
   - ONE PAST "I HAVE SUNG" 93
   - TIPS 94
   - GENERAL VOCABULARY 96
     - *The verb "ir" (= to go)* 96
     - *Remember "estar," (= to be -temporal, Chapter 7 Conjugation)* 96
     - *The verb "haber" (= to have, as an auxiliary verb)* ... 96
   - MEDICAL VOCABULARY 97
     - *Fluids, vessels, glands, and tissues* 97

10. **IRREGULARITIES IN FUTURE, PRESENT, AND PAST** ... 98
    - IRREGULAR VERBS IN THE INFINITIVE (TO SING) 99
    - IRREGULAR VERBS IN THE GERUND (SINGING) 99
    - IRREGULAR VERBS IN THE PAST PARTICIPLE (SUNG) 102
    - TIPS 102
    - GENERAL VOCABULARY 103
      - *Conjunctions* 104
    - MEDICAL VOCABULARY 105
      - *Elements, chemicals, and nutrients* 105

11. GRAMMAR RULES 106
   GENERAL VOCABULARY 116
      Possessive pronouns 116
      Object pronouns 116
      Pronouns with the preposition "con" (= with) 116
      Pronouns with other prepositions, e.g. para (= for) 116
   MEDICAL VOCABULARY 117
      Symtoms 117

12. NEGATIONS AND QUESTIONS 118
   NEGATIVE SENTENCES 118
   INTERROGATIVE SENTENCES 119
   INTERROGATIVE-NEGATIVE SENTENCES 119
   GENERAL VOCABULARY 120
      Adverbs for negations and questions 120
   MEDICAL VOCABULARY 121
      Tools and procedures of diagnostics 121

SECTION IV   VERBS

13. VERY IMPORTANT VERBS 124
   "SER" AND "ESTAR" (= TO BE) 124
   "HABER" AND "TENER" (= TO HAVE) 125
   "IR" (= TO GO) 126
   "HAY" AND "QUEDA" (= THERE IS AND THERE IS LEFT) 126
   "PODER" (= CAN, MAY) AND "TENER QUE" (= TO HAVE TO) 127
   "DEBER" (= TO OUGHT TO) AND "NECESITAR" (= TO NEED) 128
   IRREGULAR VERBS 129
   GENERAL VOCABULARY 130
      Elements of a hospital room 130
      Elements of a hospital 131
   MEDICAL VOCABULARY 132
      Disorders and diseases 132

14. TRANSLATING "IT APPEALS TO ME" 134
   THE OPTIONAL EMPHASIS IN THE PERSON 135
   THE ORDER OF THE SENTENCE 136
   TIPS 136
   GENERAL VOCABULARY 137
      Useful verbs of the gustar family 137
      Administrative data 138

MEDICAL VOCABULARY *139*
   Drugs *139*
   Tools of treatment and prevention *139*

15. **REFLEXIVITY AND PASSIVE VOICE** *140*

  REFLEXIVITY *141*
  THE PASSIVE VOICE *143*
  TIPS: *143*
  GENERAL VOCABULARY *144*
    Some verbs that can function as reflexive *144*
  MEDICAL VOCABULARY *145*
    Procedures of treatment *145*

16. **THE PRESENT AND PAST TENSES** *146*

  REGULAR VERBS IN THE PRESENT TENSE *147*
  REGULAR VERBS IN THE PAST TENSE *148*
  FALSE-IRREGULAR OR SPELLING-CHANGING VERBS ... *148*
  THE IRREGULAR VERBS *150*
  GENERAL VOCABULARY *152*
    General Questions *152*
  MEDICAL VOCABULARY *153*
    Accidents and incidents *153*
    Units *153*

17. **NEXT STEPS IN SPANISH** *154*

  WHAT HAVE YOU LEARNED *154*
  WHAT TO REMEMBER *155*
  WHAT IS OUT THERE *157*
  TIPS *158*
  GENERAL VOCABULARY *159*
    Adjectives used with "ser:" conditions *159*
    Adjectives used with "estar:" states *159*
    Verbs *160*
  MEDICAL VOCABULARY *161*
    Miscellaneous nouns *161*
    Adjectives *162*

PHRASEBOOK *164*

  GETTING A HISTORY *165*
  ASSESSMENT / DIAGNOSIS *170*
  PROCEDURES *173*
  TEACHING / FOLLOW UP *173*

APPENDICES

APPENDIX A: NOTES ABOUT DIALECTS 180
APPENDIX B: NOTES ABOUT CULTURE 186
APPENDIX C: PRESENT TENSE 192
APPENDIX D: TABLE OF ENDINGS OF THE REGULAR VERBS. 204

INDEX OF GRAMMATICAL WORDS 208
INDEX OF TECHNICAL WORDS 216

INTRODUCTION
INTRODUCCIÓN

Spanish for Health Care is intended for self-educated students with no previous knowledge of the language.

Its methodology takes advantage of the similarities between Spanish and English. Students will find motivation by realizing they are progressing, and they can speed up their learning by studying at their own pace, creating their own vocabulary, and observing sentences in clear examples. A significant percentage of English words have a Latin root, as do many structures. Spanish is derived from the Latin Language. This commonality is utilized extensively in this book to teach the Spanish language, its grammatical rules, and its coherence and consistency. For this reason, most of the Spanish words that the reader will find in this book are similar in English and, consequently, self-explanatory (as computador, pulmonar, or hospital).

The goal of this book is for professionals to be able to communicate with Spanish-speaking patients. This book will introduce the dialogue in order to understand symptoms, to convey diagnostics and medical instructions, such as referrals to specialists, prescriptions, procedures, etc. At the end of this book, you will be able to read and write any text, to convey most messages, and be able to understand substantial Spanish.

This volume presents both a textbook and a phrasebook together. The phrasebook is found before the appendices, and it shows a compilation of useful model sentences. The textbook is comprised with a set of lessons with the grammar explanation of those model sentences.

This textbook teaches the basics of the language, and shows how to become self-educated in Spanish: how to develop vocabulary efficiently, and how to find resources for your next-steps in the language. The book is engineered to be the perfect introduction to the complete grammar book *Spanish for Californians: Using English to Learn Spanish.*

This book sticks to what constitutes standard Spanish. Spanish is a very unified language. The rules of spelling and grammar are the same in all of the Spanish speaking countries, and twenty two National Academies, including those of the United States, Puerto Rico and the Philippines, work to maintain this unity.

The sections of the textbook correspond to goals. All languages have the same three components: a set of individual sounds, or **letters**, which are grouped to form **words**, which, in turn, are grouped to form **sentences**.

SOUNDS:	letters
VOCABULARY:	words
GRAMMAR:	sentences

Accordingly, the **sections** are:

Section I, SOUNDS, introduces and explains the elemental sounds. Spanish is very simple in terms of pronunciation and spelling; so simple that, at the end of Section I, you will be able to read in Spanish (though you won't know yet what you are saying).

Section II, WORDS, explains the rules that you need in order to learn words efficiently and expand your personal dictionary. English and Spanish have many words in common. This section shows how the words changes depending on being singular or plural, masculine or feminine, or referring to the past, present or future. These chapters show how words change their form (e.g. lion, lioness, lions, lionesses). At the end of Section II, you will be able to look up any word in the dictionary and start your own vocabulary list without mistakes.

Section III, SENTENCES, gives you the norms that you need in order to create and understand sentences. Spanish and English have many similarities in grammar. At the end of Section III, you will know how to create sentences using only three basic verb structures: "I am doing," "I have done," and "I am going to do."

Section IV, VERBS, provides additional information about the nucleus of the sentence: the verb. This section includes some verbs to give commands and instructions, as well as verbs with special characteristics.

Every chapter of the textbook will display:

- **The lesson**, with: language patterns, examples, golden rules and warnings .

- **Tips**, Frequently Asked Questions or Exercises

- **General Vocabulary**. All words are sorted in alphabetical order English to speed up your search.

  Words may have a mark indicating their point of stress to facilitate pronunciation. Exceptions are words as "fax" (one-vowel words) or "módem" (words with accent mark).

  Regarding which vocabulary (technical or not) to learn, we encourage you to learn a consistent set of words per day (say, ten). Some words are imposed by the language, like in English "a," "the," "to," "but," etc. Other words should come from your area of interest; those are the words that should make your learning process fun. Anyway, you should wait until completing *Chapter 8 How to Learn Words Efficiently*, to learn vocabulary in a systematic fashion.

  An index of the General Vocabulary (the grammatical words) is provided at the end of the book.

- **Medical Vocabulary**. These lists are sorted in English to speed up your search.

  As in the General Vocabulary, words may have a mark indicating their point of stress to facilitate pronunciation.

  All words of the Technical Vocabulary (with the exception of those of the last chapter) are nouns. This means that they have gender. To mark this, words not ending in "o" or "a", are preceded by "el" or "la." e.g. (el) cable, (la) construcción.

The topics of the technical vocabulary are the following:

Chapter 1	Samples of similar words
Chapter 2	Systems
Chapter 3	Medical Specialties
Chapter 4	Specialists
Chapter 5	Parts of the head
Chapter 6	Parts of the body
Chapter 7	Organs
Chapter 8	Bones
Chapter 9	Fluids, vessels, glands, and tissues
Chapter 10	Elements, chemicals, and nutrients
Chapter 11	Symtoms
Chapter 12	Tools and procedures of diagnostics
Chapter 13	Disorders and diseases
Chapter 14	Drugs / Tools of treatments
Chapter 15	Procedures of teatments
Chapter 16	Accidents and incidents/ Units
Chapter 17	Miscellaneous nouns/ Adjectives

An index of the Technical Vocabulary is provided at the end of the book.

The Phrasebook is the second part of this volume. It translates a set of useful sentences. It is classified into four main stages:

- Getting a history
- Assessment / diagnosis
- Procedures
- Teaching / follow up

Finally, four appendices supplement this book:

APENDIX A. Notes about Dialects
APENDIX B. Notes about Culture
APENDIX C. Present Tense
APENDIX D. Table of Endings of the Regular Verbs

Without further ado, here is the *Spanish for Health Care*.

SECTION I

SOUNDS
SONIDOS

In this section, you'll learn how to pronounce all of the letters in the Spanish alphabet. First, you will learn the sounds of the vowels a, e, i, o, u, and then the rest (the consonants). You will then learn the basic rules of spelling.

Later, we'll introduce "word stress," the part of the word where the emphasis falls (e.g. the "a" in actress), and its representation, the accent mark. By knowing the basic rules on the accents, you will be able to pronounce all words correctly.

By the end of this section, you will be able to read any text properly.

1. THE ALPHABET
EL ALFABETO

Spanish has the same alphabet as English, which means that they use the same symbols (letters), and that they are sorted in the same order:

a b c d e f g h i j k l m n ñ o p q r s t u v w x y z

Spanish has only one extra letter: letter "ñ." This is placed after the letter "n." This is the letter of words like "jalapeño" or "piñata." It sounds like the French "gn"(e.g. cognac, filet mignon). It sounds similar to the "n" in "onion", "bunion," or "minion; and also close to the English "nj" in injection).

Golden Rule

> In Spanish, each letter or pair of letters (like "ch" or "qu") corresponds to one sound.

For example, in Spanish, letter "a" always sounds the same (like the "a" in father); in English, letter "a" sounds differently in "father," "cable" or "salt."

Thus, pronouncing a word in Spanish is as simple as pronouncing its letters one by one. For example, in Spanish, "cable" (= cable) sounds as c + a + b + l + e (/kábleh/).

This makes Spanish one of the simplest languages in the world, and convenient particularly for self-learners.
Sounds (or "letters," to simplify) are classified mainly by **vowels**, represented by the letters: a, e, i, o, u; and **consonants**, the rest: b, c, d, f,

1. THE ALPHABET

g, etc. Vowels are articulated solely by varying the openness of your mouth. The consonants require other organs: lips, teeth, tongue, palate, larynx, etc.

Other Symbols

Different symbols that you will see are: the beginning of exclamations (¡) and the beginning of questions (¿):

>Hi!   Are you Pedro?
>¡Hola! ¿Eres Pedro?

Spanish has also a symbol to mark where the stress of the word is. In English this symbol only appears in foreign-origin words, e.g. "résumé." We'll talk about this in *Chapter 4 Accent*. For now you only need to know that all Spanish words have one, and only one, point of stress or emphasis, but this stress is not always indicated with an accent mark. This is why this book will use the underscore in those words. (e.g. ¡H_o_la! ¿_E_res P_e_dro?).

<u>Tips</u>

Frequently Asked Question

FAQ: Why in my dictionary are "ch" and "ll" considered single letters?

>Considering "ch" and "ll" as single letters is an old rule not in use any more.
>
>In old dictionaries letter "ch" is placed after letter "c," and "ll" is placed after letter "l."

General Vocabulary

The names of the letters in the alphabet

Spanish is very phonetic, consequently in Spanish it is not common to spell out words. It is a good exercise to learn the alphabet though, in order to start getting familiar with the sounds (you will learn that in the next two chapters). Realize that every name of a letter has the sound of the letter, e.g. B /beh/.

Symbol	Spanish	English Pronuntiation
A	a	ah
B	be *	beh
C	ce	ceh
D	de	deh
E	e	eh
F	efe	eh-feh
G	ge	heh
H	hache	ah-cheh
I	i	ee
J	jota	ho-tah
K	ka	kah
L	ele	eh-leh
M	eme	eh-meh
N	ene	eh-neh
Ñ	eñe	eh-gneh
O	o	oh
P	pe	peh
Q	cu	koo
R	erre	eh-rreh
S	ese	eh-seh
T	te	teh
U	u	oo
V	uve *	oo-beh
W	uve doble *	oo-beh doh-bleh
X	equis	eh-kis
Y	ye *	yeh
Z	zeta	zeh-tah

(*) Other names are used, e.g. B is also called "be larga."

1. THE ALPHABET

Medical Vocabulary

Samples of Spanish medical words that are similar in English

Since you have not learned how to pronounce the Spanish letters yet, we'll start the vocabulary section of this book with samples of words and their silmilarities with English. You will also find the words of this section in their corresponding chapter.

First, there are words English-origin words that have become part of Spanish and that are **written and pronounced as in English**. These words are written in *italic* to indicate that they must be pronounced as those of the original language . Some examples are: camping, campus, email, hardware, hobby, ipad, Kleenex, OK, piercing, sandwich, software.

Commonly English and Spanish scientific words come from Latin (the language which Spanish comes from), and you can expect many words are similar in both languages.

A few Spanish words are **identical** to English (same spelling, pronunciation and stress). Examples are:

English	= Spanish
colon	
coma	
gas	
placenta	

A few Spanish words **differ in the spelling** from their English counterparts, but they are pronounced the same. Examples are:

English	Spanish
asthma	asma
asphyxia	asfixia
bypass	baipás
cancer	cáncer

Some Spanish words differ **in the stress,** but spelling and pronunciation are the same that their English conteparts. Examples are:

English	Spanish
abdomen	abd_o_men
dental	dent_a_l
doctor	doct_o_r
epidural	epidur_a_l

> **Note**: This book uses the underscore to indicate the stress. Also notice that, unlike English, Spanish words ending in "al," "ar," "or," tend to have the stress in the last syllable.

Some Spanish words **differ in the pronounciation** but they are spelt the same. Examples are:

English	Spanish	
hospital	hospit_a_l	/os-pee-tal/
gel	gel	/hell/
nasal	nas_a_l	/nah-sal/
virus	v_i_rus	/bee-roos/

Most Spanish technical words that are **recognizable** from an English speaker. These words are called "cognates" in English ("cognados" in Spanish). Examples of these words are abundant.

English	Spanish
analysis	análisis
appendix	apéndice
bacterium	bact_e_ria
biopsy	bi_o_psia
diagnostics	diagnóstico
fever	fi_e_bre
inflammation	inflamación
intestine	intest_i_no
larynx	lar_i_nge
microscope	microsc_o_pio
prostate	próstata
rectum	r_e_cto

1. THE ALPHABET

English	Spanish
stomach	estómago
suture	sut<u>u</u>ra
vertebra	vértebra

As you will read in *Chapter 8 How to Learn Words Efficiently*, the effective vocabulary is that that comes from your experience. Only you know the words that you will use at work. In this section you will find sets of words grouped by topics, where you can start building your own dictionary.

2. THE VOWELS
LAS VOCALES

The vowel sounds in Spanish are represented by the letters a, e, i, o, u.

Letter	Sound
a	like the "a" of father
e	like the "e" of bed
i	like the "ea" of meat
o	like the "o" of open
u	like the "oo" of boot

Use this rule of thumb to memorize the sounds: they sound in English like: ah, eh, ih, oh, uh.

Warning

> Be aware that some letters, including the vowels, **don't sound identical** in both languages, but they are **close enough**. (English has a much wider range of sounds than Spanish, which gives English speakers an advantage as learners). With practice you will perfect your pronunciation.

For example, the English "oo" of "good" is slightly longer than the Spanish "u." Differences like this make the learner have an accent in Spanish. Those adjustments to the new language occur fast (and for the most part unconsciously) when trying to imitate the native speakers.

2. THE VOWELS

For now what is important is that you remember that the Spanish a, e, i, o, u always sound the same. On the contrary, in English, "a," for instance, sounds differently in "**a**pple" and "**a**pe."

Remember that every letter sounds independently. Thus, the combination of them must be pronounced accordingly. Examples:

>león = l +e + o +n (= lion)
>día = d + i +a (= day)

The letter "u" is silent when preceded by "q," or when preceded by "g." Examples:

>Quito = k + i + t + o (= Quito)
>guitarra = g + i + t + a + r r + a ("g" like in "guitar")

Following this idea, if you have two vowels together, you must pronounce both. So, in Spanish, the name "Aaron" must sound as: a+a+r+o+n.

Tips

Exercise

Pronounce the Spanish words: Asia, cable, euro and pus (They have the same meaning in English).

When you pronounce them, if they sound like they do in English, then you did something wrong... They should sound:

>a + s + i + a
>c + a + b + l + e
>e + u + r o
>p + u + s

General Vocabulary

Numbers from 0 to 10

Symbol	Spanish Spelling	English Pronuntiation *
0	cero **	c<u>e</u>h-roh
1	uno	<u>oo</u>-noh
2	dos	dos
3	tres	tres
4	cuatro	kw<u>a</u>-troh
5	cinco	c<u>ee</u>n-coh
6	seis	s<u>eh</u>-ees
7	siete	see-<u>e</u>h-teh
8	ocho	<u>o</u>h-choh
9	nueve	nw<u>e</u>h-beh
10	diez	dee-<u>e</u>hs

(*) In the next chapter, you will learn the phonetic value of the rest of the letters of the alphabet, and you will see that, in Spanish, every word is pronounced as a sequence of individual letters (sounds).

(**) As a reminder, never forget that the strongest tool that you have to memorize words in Spanish is their similarities with English. Always question yorself if the word you are going to memorize ressembles a word in English. For example, think of these words related to the table above: **tri**angle (3), **quart**er (4), **octo**pus (8), **deci**mal (10).

A single word with all vowels

There are very few words that have all the vowels. Since the vowels always sound the same (with the exception of the mute "u" in the pair "gu" and "qu"), it is worthwhile memorizing one that you can resort to when you are learning the sounds of the vowels.

An example of this is "murciélago" /moor-see-eh-lah-goh/, or simpler:

m + u + r + c + i + e + l + a + g + o

2. THE VOWELS

Medical Vocabulary

Systems

English	Spanish
circulatory system	aparato circulatorio
digestive system	aparato digestivo
endocrine system	aparato endocrino
excretory system	aparato excretor
integumentary system	aparato integumentario
lymphatic system	aparato linfático
musculoskeletal system	aparato locomotor
nervous systems	aparato nervioso
reproductive system	aparato reproductor
respiratory system	aparato respiratorio

Notes:

1. Pay attention to the pronunciation of vowels, according to the rules learned in this chapter. Also pay attention to the combinations of vowels, as "io," in circulatorio or nervioso.

2. As you will learn in *Chapter 6 Masculine/ Feminine*, in Spanish all nouns have gender (Nouns are the words that defines beings and objects, as John, cat, lamp or system). As a general rule all words ending in "o" are masculine, as "aparato." Thus "the system" will be "el aparato" (not "la aparato").

3. THE CONSONANTS
LAS CONSONANTES

The consonants are those letters (sounds) that are not vowels. They are:

Letter	Sound	Examples in Spanish
b	As in English.	Bolivia
c	**Two possible sounds:** When followed by *a, o, u* (ca, co, cu) or by a consonant (cr, cl) it sounds as the hard "c" in English Otherwise, it sounds like the the "c" in "cement." Only in Spain, it sounds like the "th" in "thing"	→ capital, coma, curioso, crema, clase (= capital, comma, curious, cream, class) → cemento, cine (= cement, cinema)
d	Softer than in English.	diamante (= diamond)
f	As in English.	Filipinas (= Philippines)
g	**Two possible sounds:** 1. As the guttural "g" in English, when "g" is followed by *a, o, u* (ga, go, gu, gue, gui) or a consonant (gl, gr) 2. Otherwise (ge, gi), it sounds as the "h" in "hippo"	→ gala, golf, gurú, guerrilla, guitarra, glándula, gris (= gala, golf, guru, guerilla, guitar, gland, gray) → general, gigante (= general, giant)

3. THE CONSONANTS

Letter	Sound	Examples in Spanish
h	Silent unless combined in "ch"	hora (= hour)
j	As the English "h" in "ham, Helen, hipo or home"	San José
k	As in English	kilogramo (= kilogram)
l	As in English	lámpara (= lamp)
m	As in English	médico (= doctor)
n	As in English	Nicaragua
ñ	Like the "gn" of "cognac"	coñac (= cognac)
p	As in English	Perú
q	As is English (In Spanish, q is always followed by u)	Quito
r	**Two possible sounds:** 1. As the English "r," if not at the beginning of the word 2. At the beginning of a word, or paired, it sounds stronger (see next page)	→ hora (= hour) → rápido, carro (= rapid, car)
s	As in English	sonido (= sound)
t	As in English	Tijuana
v	As the English "b"	Venezuela
w	As in English	waterpolo (= waterpolo)
x	As in English	examen (= exam)
y	**Two possible sounds.** 1. It sounds as "ea" of "meal," when at the end of words or isolated (meaning "and") 2. Otherwise, it sounds as the English "j" in "jam"	→ y (= and), Uruguay → mayor (= major)
z	As the "c" in "cement." Only in Spain, it sounds like the English "th" in "thing"	zoología (= zoology)

Remember:

Letters **b** and **v** both sound like English "b."

Letter c has two sounds. In "**ce**," "**ci**," letter c sounds like in English. Only in Spain, it sounds as the th of **th**under. Otherwise, in "**ca, co, cu, cr, cl**," it sounds like in English (like a "k").

Letter d is weaker than that of English. In Spanish "d" sounds especially weak when it's placed between vowels. Thus the words "cansado" (= tired) is pronounced "cansao" by some speakers.

Letter g has two sounds (as it does in English). In **ga, go, gu** sounds like the g in the English **ga**rage, **go**vernment, **gu**ru. Also like English, the combination **gue, gui** will sound: guerilla and guitar. This very sound is the one for the combinations gl, gr, like in gland, grand. However ge, gi sound like the Spanish "j" of "San José," which is a stronger than the English "h" of "ham."

Letter h is silent. However **ch** is pronounced like English of "China."

Letter ñ doesn't exist in English as a letter. However the sound is in popular words like "piñata," "jalapeño" or "el niño" (the atmospheric phenomenon). It sounds like the gn in co**gn**ac or filet mi**gn**on (close to the "nj" in i**nj**ection).

Letter q can only be found in the combination with "u" to form: **que, qui**. sounding as "k." Thus, the two spellings kilo and quilo result in the same pronunciation.

Letter r has two pronunciations: weak and strong r (simple and multiple vibrating r). The weak sound corresponds to that of the English "r." The strong r is represented either by the single letter r when in the beginning of the word or by "rr." English doesn't have this sound. The strong r sound has the same articulation as the weak r but the tongue vibrates (similar to the onomatopoeia "brrr" or "grrr").

Letter y has two sounds. One as the Spanish vowel "i," (the English "ea" of meal") when meaning "and," or when at the end of a word, like "Paraguay." Otherwise it sounds as the English "j" in "jam."

Letter z sounds as the "c" of "ceremony". Only in Spain, it sounds as the "th" of **th**under.

3. THE CONSONANTS

In addition, "**ch, ll, rr**" have one single sound each:

Pair	Sound	Examples in Spanish
ch	As in English.	Chile
ll	As the English "j" in joke.	llama (= flame)
rr	As the English "r," but it vibrates multiple times.	carro (= car)

Notice that only the **sounds** of the Spanish "ñ," "j," and the strong "r" are foreign in English. Try to pronounce the model words: co**gn**ac, **S**an **J**osé, and "**brrr**!" Especially "**rr**" is a challenge for foreigners. Take time to learn to pronounce it.

Also notice that some letters have the same sound in Spanish. These are the pairs: b/v, ll/y, and j/g (ge, gi). These, together with the silent letter "h," become a problem of **spelling**. Examples:

> gobernar (not ~~governar~~), general (not ~~jeneral~~), fallar (not ~~fayar~~), humano (not ~~umano~~)
> (= to govern, general, to fail, human)

Regarding the pairs of consonants in the same syllable. Spanish only admits:

bl	cl	~~dl~~	fl	gl	pl	tl *
br	cr	dr	fr	gr	pr	tr

(*) Very rarely found

Notice that all of them have either "l" or "r" as the second letter of the pair.

Examples:

blusa	clon	---	Florida	glaciar	planta	nauatl
brillo	acre	dragón	Francia	gran	primer	trío

Which mean:

blouse	clone	---	Florida	glacier	plant	nauatl
brightness	acre	dragon	France	great	first	trio

Spanish doesn't have **the sounds** for the English "sh" and "sr" (sheet, Sri Lanka).

Spanish doesn't have the pair of **letters** "ck." For that **sound**, Spanish uses: "c," "qu" or "k." Spanish doen't have "ph," only "f." Examples:

>ro**ck**, che**ck**, ele**ph**ant
>ro**c**a, che**qu**e, ele**f**ante

Likewise, Spanish does not have the English pairs of **letters** bb, dd, ff, mm, pp, ss, tt or zz. For those **sounds**, Spanish uses a single letter. Examples:

>ro**bb**ery, a**dd**itional, di**ff**erence, mo**mm**y, a**pp**lication, cla**ss**,
>lo**tt**ery, pu**zz**le
>ro**b**o, a**d**icional, di**f**erencia, ma**m**á, a**p**licación, cla**s**e,
>lo**t**ería, pu**z**le.

Warning

In Spanish you may find cc, mb, mp, etc., but each letter of the pair belongs to a different syllable. E.g. **ac-t**or, **ac-c**ión, a-**dic-t**o, e-le-**fan-t**e (= actor, action, addict, elephant)

Now, with the rules explained, you can read any word and write (maybe misspelling) any word. The only thing left to be able to read is to learn where the stress is placed on each word, which constitutes the next chapter, *Chapter 4 Accent*.

Rules of Thumb on Spelling

Some basic rules can help you guess the right spelling (remember that there's no set of rules that covers all cases for the indistinguishable pairs v/b, g/j, ll/y, and the h).

>1) Pairs "bb, dd, ff, pp, ss, tt, zz" don't exist.
>E.g. abreviación, not ~~abbreviación~~; efecto, not ~~effecto~~; adicción*, not ~~addiccion~~. (= effect; abbreviation, addiction)
>(*) Notice that the cc is, in reality, c-c, e.g. a-dic-ción

3. THE CONSONANTS

2) Words can't start with letter "s" followed by a consonant.
E.g. especial (= special), not ~~special~~ .

3) K and W are very rarely used (karate, kimono, okey –OK-, waterpolo, Washington and a few more). Use "c" or "q" for the k sound; and use: "gua, güe, güi, guo, gu" for the w-sound.

4) Use "ce," "ci," instaead of "ze," "zi."
E.g. cero, not ~~zero~~ (as in English).

5) The plural of words ending in -z, is -ces, not –zes.
E.g. cruz → cruces, not ~~cruzes~~ (= cross)

6) M (not n) goes before b or p.
E.g. bomba (= bomb or pump), not ~~bomva.~~

7) Words of the same family have similar spelling.
E.g. **h**ombre, **h**umano, **h**umanizar, **h**umanidades
(= man, human, humanize, humanities)

8) Words **ending** with "i" vowel sound in Spanish are spelled: ay, ey, oy, uy (not ai, ei, oi, ui), when the stress is not in the last vowel.
E.g. Paragu_ay_, ahí, r_ey_, reí, l_ey_, leí, h_oy_, oí, huy, huí
(= Paraguay, there, king, I laughed, law, I read (past), today, I heard, ouch!, I fled).

9) Words starting with vowel sound "ua," "ue," "ui," "ia," and "ie" are spelled with "h:" hua, hue, hui, hia, hie.
E.g. Huáscar, huevo, huir, hiato, hielo
(= Huascar, egg, to flee, hiatus, ice).

Tips

Frequently Asked Questions

FAQ 1: Why have I never heard the English "th" sound in Spanish?

> Using the "s" sound instead of "th" sound is also accepted. This use is found in Latin America, including Mexico and the US (See *Appendix A: Notes About Dialects*).

FAQ 2: What are the two dots on the "u" in "lingüista?"

> Words like lingüista or pingüino (= linguist, penguin) have this symbol called dieresis (diéresis, in Spanish). We saw that in the combination "gue" or "gui" the "u" is silent. To spell a word where the "u" needs to sound, you need dieresis. It is also used in English by some newspapers to mark that a certain letter must be pronounced, like "coöperation" (the "oo" would sound like in boot, otherwise). Spanish uses this symbol with the same intent: to mark that the "u" must be pronounced.

FAQ 3: I've seen both "México" and "Méjico." What's the right spelling?

> Both. The Spanish words México, Nuevo México, Texas and Oaxaca (and very few others) can be spelled with "x" or with "j." The **Mexican** Academy of Spanish Language decided to spell it with "x" for historical reasons. In any case, it is pronounced as a Spanish "j" sound. In the rest of the Spanish speaking countries, these words are spelled with "j" (Méjico, Nuevo Méjico, Tejas, Oajaca).

FAQ 4: Should "y" and "ll" sound the same?

> Originally "ll" sounded as the English "ll" in "million" (It still sounds this way in some places in Spain and Bolivia). With time, "ll" acquired the sound of the "y." **Nowadays** both "y" and "ll" sound the same. On the other hand, there are variations in the way Spanish speakers pronounce y. In Argentina, it sounds especially strong (See *Appendix A: Notes About Dialects*).

FAQ 5: I have heard that some people don't pronounce the "s." Is this optional?

> This is a mispronunciation. This is not standard Spanish. Every region of the Spanish speaking world has their own "popular" deviations from the standard. This is one: many people in the Caribbean omit the "s" not placed at the beginning of the word. Examples:
>
> Standard Spanish: dos, tres, es-tó-ma-go, no-so-tros
> Non Standard Spanish: do' , tre', e'tómago, no-'o-tro'
> English: two, three, stomach, we

3. THE CONSONANTS

Exercises

a) Pronounce the Spanish words:

> Pu<u>e</u>rto R<u>i</u>co
> Est<u>a</u>dos Un<u>i</u>dos (= United States)
> Calif<u>o</u>rnia
> Nu<u>e</u>vo Méjico, Nu<u>e</u>vo Méjico (same pronunciation)
> T<u>e</u>jas, T<u>e</u>xas (same pronunciation)
> Color<u>a</u>do
> Ariz<u>o</u>na
> Nev<u>a</u>da
> Flor<u>i</u>da (not Fl<u>o</u>rida)
> Norteamérica (= North America)
> Suramérica (= South America)
> Centroamérica (= Central America)

b) Pronounce the Spanish words:

> general (same meanings as in English: the opposite of "specific" and the military rank)
> hotel (same meaning as in English)
> zoo (same meaning as in English)

Notes:

> When you pronounce them, if they sound like they do in English, then you are doing something wrong. They should sound:
>
> g + e+ n + e + r + a + l ("g" sounds like the "J" in "San José")
> o + t + e + l ("h" is silent)
> z + o + o ("z" sounds like th; "o" sounds twice)

General Vocabulary

Spanish-speaking Countries

In *Chapter 8 How to Learn Words Efficiently*, you'll have the tools to start developing your own vocabulary. Until then, you can take advantage that some names of places are the same or very similar in Spanish and English.

Remember, although words can look the same in both languages, in Spanish, they sound as letter by letter.

Spanish
Argentina
Bolivia
Chile
Colombia
Costa Rica
Cuba
República Dominicana (Dominican Republic)
Ecuador
El Salvador
Guatemala
Honduras
México/ Méjico
Nicaragua
Panamá
Paraguay
Perú
España (Spain)
Uruguay
Venezuela

Note: The countries are commonly feminine (e.g. la Argentina) feminine), however typically the article el/ la (the) is not used, consequently, you don't need to know their gender.

3. THE CONSONANTS

Medical Vocabulary

Medical specialties

English	Spanish
medical specialties	(las) especialidades médicas
anesthesiology	anestesiología
cardiology	cardiología
dentistry	odontología
dermatology	dermatología
ENT (ear, nose and throat)	otorrinolaringología
gastroenterology	gastroenterología
geriatrics	geriatría
gynecology	ginecología
internal medicine	medicina interna
kinesiology	kinesiología, quinesiología
medicine	medicina
neurology	neurología
nursing	enfermería
obstetrics	obstetricia
oncology	oncología
ophthalmology	oftalmología
pediatrics	pediatría
pharmacy	farmacia
pediatrics	pediatría
psychiatry	psiquiatría
psychology	psicología
physical therapy	fisioterapia
pulmonology	neumología
radiology	radiología
social work	trabajo social
surgery	cirugía
therapy	terapia
traumatology	traumatología
urology	urología

As you will learn in *Chapter 6 Masculine/ Feminine*, all Spanish nouns have gender. As a general rule, all words ending in "a" are feminine, as "dermatología," or "medicina." In this book, words following this rule don't have the indication "la," e.g. la especialidad

4. ACCENT
ACENTO

So far, you know how to pronounce the sound of a word but not the right intonation of it. It's not the same to say "dess__er__t" and "d__e__sert," or __i__mport and imp__or__t. Every word has a point of emphasis or stress.

All Spanish words have one and only one point of stress, and this always falls on a vowel -never on a consonant, e.g. (underscored)

        __a__sma, v__e__na, digest__i__vo, abd__o__men, vac__u__na
        asthma, vein, digestive, abdomen, vaccine

Spanish uses the accent mark (á, é, í, ó, ú) to indicate where the stress is.

        análisis, alérgico, clínica, estómago, útero
        analysis, allergic, clinic, stomach, uterus

Although all words have a point of stress, not all words have an accent mark, as you can see in the first series above: __a__sma, v__e__na, digest__i__vo, abd__o__men, vac__u__na.

This book uses the underline to indicate where the stress of a word is when the accent mark is not used.

4. ACCENT

Golden Rule

> All words, with no exception, have one, and only one, point of **stress**, and this always falls on a vowel (never on a consonant). The **accent marks** (á, é, í, ó, ú) indicate where the stressed vowel is. However, the majority of words don't require an **accent mark**.

Notice that many Spanish words that look similar to English, have a different point of stress:

>   hospital, alergia, dentista, tendón, único
>   hospital, allergy, dentist, tendon, unique

Rule of Thumb on Stress

There is a rule to help you know where the stress is when you read a word: all words that have the stress in the third to last syllable or before must have an accent mark. Examples:

>   sá-ba-do, tó-rri-do, có-li-co, diag-nós-ti-co, ór-ga-no *
>   saturday, torrid, colic, diagnostics, organ

>   (*) dashes above are just to indicate the breakdown into syllables

In addition to this, the majority of words in Spanish have the stress in the second to last syllable.

If you combine both (the actual rule and the tendency), the resulting rule of thumb is: if a word doesn't have an accent mark, it **most likely** has the stress in the second to last syllable. Example:

>   so-pa, com-pu-ta-do-ra, pel-vis, bron-qui-is, cor-te, ac-ci-den-te
>   soup, computer, pelvis, bronchitis, cut, accident

Tips

Frequently Asked Questions

FAQ 1: Vídeo or Video?

> A few words can be pronounced with different stress. This is the case of vídeo/ vid_eo (= video, video tape, DVR). In Mexico vid_eo is preferred.
>
> Another word is período/peri_odo (= period). You choose.

FAQ 2: What is the difference between accent mark and stress?

> Stress is the elevation of intonation of a vowel in the word. An accent mark is the mark that indicates that stress. In Spanish, every word has one (and only one) stressed vowel; however, most of the words don't have an accent mark. The term "accent" is confusing since it may mean either "stress" or "accent mark." Normally "accent" refers to "accent mark."
>
> This book uses the underline to mark the stress in those words that have no accent mark.

FAQ 3: Do I need to learn the rules for the accent marks?

> Yes and no. You need to if you want to know where the stress is in any word in the dictionary; in order to communicate in a written form, you don't need it. Any Spanish reader will understand your written notes without accent marks.

FAQ 4: I have seen the word "él" and "el," so the same word with and without accent mark. Which one is correct?

> The accent mark is also used to distinguish words that have the same pronunciation and spelling but that can be ambiguous. So, "él" means "he," in English, and "el," "the". Other example is "sí" (= yes) , and "si" (=if).
>
> There is just a few words that have accent for this reason. The majority of words that have more than one meaning are not distinguished with the accent mark, e.g. hoja (= leaf, paper).

4. ACCENT

General Vocabulary

Interjections and greetings

English	Spanish
Excuse me.	Con perm<u>i</u>so./ Perdón.
Good afternoon (until dusk).	Bu<u>e</u>nas t<u>a</u>rdes.
Good evening. / Good night.	Bu<u>e</u>nas n<u>o</u>ches.
Good morning (until lunch time).	Bu<u>e</u>nos días.
Goodbye.	Adiós.
Hello.	H<u>o</u>la.
Help!	¡Ay<u>u</u>da!
I don't know.	No lo sé./ No sé.
I wish!	Ojalá.
I'm sorry.	Lo si<u>e</u>nto.
Maybe.	Tal vez./ Quizás./ Quizá.
Me neither.	Yo tamp<u>o</u>co.
Me too.	Yo también.
Okay.	<u>O</u>key.
Please.	Por fav<u>o</u>r.
Really?	¿De verd<u>a</u>d?
Right?	¿Verd<u>a</u>d?
See you later.	H<u>a</u>sta la v<u>i</u>sta.
See you later.	H<u>a</u>sta lu<u>e</u>go.
See you soon.	H<u>a</u>sta pr<u>o</u>nto.
Thank you.	Gr<u>a</u>cias.
Thank you very much.	M<u>u</u>chas Gr<u>a</u>cias.
You're welcome.	De n<u>a</u>da.

Medical Vocabulary

Specialists

English	Spanish
specialists	especialistas
anesthesiologist	(el/ la) anestesista
cardiologist	cardiólogo/ a
dentist	(el, la) dentista
dermatologist	dermatólogo/ a
doctor, physician	doctor/ a, (el/ la) médico
ENT specialist	otorrino/ otorrinolaringólogo/a
gastroenterologist	gastroenterólogo/ a
gerontologist	(el, la) geriatra
gynecologist	ginecólogo/ a
kinesiologist	kinesiólogo/ a, quinesiólogo/ a
midwife	comadrona
neurologist	neurólogo/ a
nurse	enfermero/ a
oncologist	oncólogo/ a
ophthalmologist	oftalmólogo/ a, (el/ la) oculista
paramedic	paramédico/ a
pediatrician	(el, la) pediatra
pharmacist	farmacéutico/ a
physical therapist	(el/la) fisioterapeuta
practitioner	(el/ la) médico de familia
psychiatrist	(el, la) psiquiatra
psychologist	psicólogo/ a
pulmonologist	neumólogo/ a
radiographer	radiólogo/ a
social worker	trabajador/a social
specialist	(el, la) especialista
surgeon	cirujano/ a
technician	(el, la) técnico
therapist	(el, la) terapeuta
traumatologist	traumatólogo/ a
urologist	urólogo/ a

4. ACCENT

<u>Notes</u>

In this book the undescore indicates the point of stress. Words with just one vowel or with an accent mark won't need this help.

As you will learn in *Chapter 6: Masculine/ Feminine*, Spanish nouns they all have gender. So, words as "cat" (feminine in Spanish, no matter the real gender of the cat) uses the masculine article "el," el gato (= the cat); and "lamp" (feminine in Spanish) uses the feminine article "la," la lámpara (= the lamp).

With most of the professions, as cardiólogo or dermatólogo, you will put "o" or "a" at the end, and will use "el" or "la" if the person in question is a man or a woman:

> He is the cardiologist. / She is the cardiologist.
> Él es el cardiologo./ Ella es la cardióloga.

With professions ending in "a", as "dentista" or "geriatra," the same word works for both, and you just have to put "el" or "la" accordingly.

> He is the dentist. / She is the dentist.
> Él es el dentista. / Ella es la dentista.

SECTION II

WORDS
PALABRAS

Congratulations! Now you can read and write words in Spanish.

This section will teach you how to learn the meaning of those words by looking in the dictionary. Obvious? Not really. Imagine that you want to know the meaning of the English word "appendices" (not appendix). If the dictionary doesn't include the plural of words, you would get frustrated by finding "appendix," but not "appendices."

Another example would be if you wanted to look up the English word "studied" (not: study).

This short Section II will give you a guide by discussing three topics:

    Singular/plural, also called number

    Masculine/feminine, also called gender

    Person and tense, also called conjugation

In the end of this section, you will be able to find any word in the dictionary to create your own dictionary with your own vocabulary.

5. SINGULAR / PLURAL
SINGULAR / PLURAL

Like English, Spanish has "singular/plural" (identifiers for one/more than one), and both languages use the same way to identify "more than one:" they add the letter "s."

Like in English if the noun is plural, then the word that precedes it (determiner) is also plural. The words "a," "the," "this," and "that" are called determiners.

<u>a</u> hotel,   <u>some</u> hotels
DET. NOUN   DET.   NOUN

<u>un</u> hotel,   <u>unos</u> hoteles
DET. NOUN   DET.   NOUN

this cat, these cats
este gato, estos gatos

that elephant, those elephants
ese elefante, esos elefantes

Unlike English, the determiner "the" also changes.

the planet, the planets
el planeta, los planetas

Unlike English, in Spanish if the noun is plural, the adjective (like elegant, black or enormous) is also plural.

5. SINGULAR / PLURAL

an	elegant	hotel,		some	elegant	hotels,
DET.	ADJ.	NOUN		DET.	ADJ.	NOUN

un	hotel	elegante,		unos	hoteles	elegantes
DET.	NOUN	ADJ.		DET.	NOUN	ADJ.

this black cat, these black cats (the word black does not change).
este gato negro, estos gatos negros

that enormous elephant, those enormous elephants
ese elefante enorme, esos elefantes enormes

Golden Rule

> Like English, Spanish creates the plural by adding:
> -"**s**," if the word ends in a vowel
> -"**es**," if the word ends in a consonant

Examples

    One hour, two hour**s**, three hour**s**
    Una hora, dos hora**s**, tres hora**s**

    One album, two albums, three albums
    un álbum, dos álbum**es**, tres álbum**es**

If the word ends in letter "z," then you change "z" to a "c" and add "es."
    One cross, two cros**ses**, three cros**ses**
    Una cruz, dos cru**ces**, tres cru**ces**

Only some determiners add "**os**" to create the plural. These are:

    un / unos (a/some)
    el / los (the/the -plural)
    este / estos (this/these)
    ese / esos (that/those)
    aquel / aquellos (that/those)
    algún / algunos (any/some)

Numbers

By paying attention to the series of numbers, you can easily deduce how to form any figure:

1	2	3	4	5	6	7	8	9	10
uno	dos	tres	cu_a_tro	c_i_nco	s_e_is	si_e_te	_o_cho	nu_e_ve	di_e_z

Note: underscore indicates stressed vowel.

10, 11, 12…19	20, 21, 22…29	30, 31, 32…39
diez	veinte	treinta
once	veintiuno	treinta y uno
doce	veintidós	treinta y dos
trece	veintitrés	treinta y tres
catorce	veinticuatro	treinta y cuatro
quince	veinticinco	treinta y cinco
dieciséis	veintiséis	treinta y seis
diecisiete	veintisiete	treinta y siete
dieciocho	veintiocho	treinta y ocho
diecinueve	veintinueve	treinta y nueve

40, 41, 42…49	50, 51, 52…59	60, 61, 62…69
cuarenta	cincuenta	sesenta
cuarenta y uno	cincuenta y uno	sesenta y uno
cuarenta y dos	cincuenta y dos	sesenta y dos
cuarenta y tres	cincuenta y tres	sesenta y tres
cuarenta y cuatro	cincuenta y cuatro	sesenta y cuatro
cuarenta y cinco	cincuenta y cinco	sesenta y cinco
cuarenta y seis	cincuenta y seis	sesenta y seis
cuarenta y siete	cincuenta y siete	sesenta y siete
cuarenta y ocho	cincuenta y ocho	sesenta y ocho
cuarenta y nueve	cincuenta y nueve	sesenta y nueve

5. SINGULAR / PLURAL

70, 71, 72…79	80, 81, 82…89	90, 91, 92…99
setenta	ochenta	noventa
setenta y uno	ochenta y uno	noventa y uno
setenta y dos	ochenta y dos	noventa y dos
setenta y tres	ochenta y tres	noventa y tres
setenta y cuatro	ochenta y cuatro	noventa y cuatro
setenta y cinco	ochenta y cinco	noventa y cinco
setenta y seis	ochenta y seis	noventa y seis
setenta y siete	ochenta y siete	noventa y siete
setenta y ocho	ochenta y ocho	noventa y ocho
setenta y nueve	ochenta y nueve	noventa y nueve

100	cien, ciento
200	doscientos/as
300	trescientos/as
400	cuatrocientos/as
500	quinientos/as
600	seiscientos/as
700	setecientos/as
800	ochocientos/as
900	novecientos/as
1000	mil
10,000	diez mil
100,000	cien mil
1,000,000	un millón
1,000,000,000	mil millones
100,000,000,000	cien mil millones
1,000,000,000,000	un billón

Notes about numbers

There is a distinction between "uno" and "un/una" (see next, *Chapter 6 Masculine/Feminine*). "Uno" can only be used when it refers to a number, not a quantity of something.

>twenty one; twenty one albums, twenty one hours
>veintiuno; ventiún álbumes; ventiuna horas

The word "cien" changes to "ciento" when it is not one hundred even.

>100 albums;   101 albums;   190 albums
>cien álbumes; ciento un álbumes; ciento noventa álbumes

>100,000 albums; 1,100 albums
>cien mil álbumes; mil cien álbumes

The words doscientos (200), trescientos (300),... novecientos (900) change to doscientas, trescientas, ...novecientas if the word that follows is feminine (*Chapter 6 Masculine/Feminine*).

>Five hundred people
>Quinientas personas

The word "millón" in Spanish needs the word "de" (= of), unlike English.

>100 hours; 1,000 hours; 1,000,000 hours
>cien horas; mil horas;   un millón de horas

In Spanish figures are never expressed in terms of hundreds.

>2100 = two thousand one hundred or twenty one hundred
>2100 = dos mil cien (not veintiún cientos)

"Billón" in Spanish is <u>not</u> billion in English, but 1,000,000,000,000. "Mil millones" is one billion.

5. SINGULAR / PLURAL

Telling the Time

To refer to a time or ask for the time:

> What's the time?
> ¿Qué hora es?

> **At** what time is the appointment?
> ¿**A** qué hora es la cita?

As in English there are **two forms** to tell the time:

> It's one fifteen.   = It's a quarter past one.
> Es la una y quince. = Es la una y cuarto.

One Form	The Other Form	Time
Son las doce y 45	Es la una menos cuarto.	12:45
Es la una	Es la una en punto.	1:00
Es la una y 15.	Es la una y cuarto.	1:15
Es la una y 30.	Es la una y media.	1:30
Son las dos.	Son las dos en punto.	2:00
Son las dos y 5.		2:05
Son las dos y 10.		2:10
Son las dos y 15.	Son las dos y cuarto.	2:15
Son las dos y 20.		2:20
Son las dos y 25.		2:25
Son las dos y 30.	Son las dos y media.	2:30
Son las dos y 35.	Son las tres menos 25.	2:35
Son las dos y 40.	Son las tres menos 20.	2:40
Son las dos y 45.	Son las tres menos cuarto.	2:45
Son las dos y 50.	Son las tres menos 10.	2:50
Son las dos y 55.	Son las tres menos 5.	2:55

Telling the Date

In Spanish, when telling the date, the day always precedes the month.

> What day of the week is today? Today is Saturday.
> ¿Qué día es hoy? Hoy es Sábado.

> What date is today? Today is February 21, 2007.
> ¿Qué día es hoy? Hoy es (el) 21 de Febrero de 2007.

Month	Mes
January	Enero
February	Febrero
March	Marzo
April	Abril
May	Mayo
June	Junio

Month	Mes
July	Julio
August	Agosto
September	Septiembre
October	Octubre
November	Noviembre
December	Diciembre

Tips

Frequently Asked Questions

FAQ 1: What's the plural of words like "cactus?"

> Like English, Spanish has a reduced number of words that have an irregular plural, like cactus.
>
> > un cactus, dos cactus, tres cactus
> > (= a cactus, two cacti, three cacti)
>
> In general, Spanish words ending in "–us," "–is" don't change. An exception is gris-grises (= gray).
>
> > crisis - crisis, análisis - análisis, tesis -tesis
> > (= crisis - crises, analysis - analyses, thesis - theses)
>
> Some words ending in "–í" can change to "íes," e.g. iraní, iraníes (= Iranian, Iranians).

5. SINGULAR / PLURAL   55

FAQ 2: Can I express years in hundreds?

No, in Spanish no quantity (not only years) is expressed in hundreds.

In nineteen forty (1940)...
En mil novecientos cuarenta... (not ~~En diecinueve cuarenta~~)

Exercise

Spell out the following figures:

253   153   1,101   1,929   2,128   5,100

This exercise is for you to "say" the numbers; the spelling of the figures is not important (since you always use the symbols of the numbers).

Answers

253	doscientos cincuenta y tres
153	ciento cincuenta y tres
1,101	mil ciento uno
1,929	mil novecientos veintinueve
2,128	dos mil ciento veintiocho
5,100	cinco mil cien

General Vocabulary

Days of the week

English	Spanish
Monday	lunes *
Tuesday	martes
Wednesday	miércoles
Thursday	jueves
Friday	viernes
Saturday	sábado
Sunday	domingo

(*) In Spanish, the week starts on Monday, not on Sunday.

The translation of the "on" of "**on** Monday, on Tuesday" is "**el** lunes, **el** martes…"

Months of the year

English	Spanish
January	Enero
February	Febrero
March	Marzo
April	Abril
May	Mayo
June	Junio
July	Julio
August	Agosto
September	Septiembre
October	Octubre
November	Noviembre
December	Diciembre

The translation of "in" (in January) is "en" (en Enero).

The translation of "first" of January is "el uno" de Enero (literally: the one of Enero). Notice that Spanish doesn't use the ordinals (first, second, third…) for dates, as English does (e.g. first of June).

5. SINGULAR / PLURAL

Time units (in natural order)

English	Spanish
year	a̲ño
month	(el) mes
week	sem̲ana
day	día
hour	ho̲ra
minute	minu̲to
second	segu̲ndo

Other words to express time

English	Spanish
and	y
date	fe̲cha
half	me̲dia
is	es
minus	me̲nos
of	de
quarter (1/4)	cua̲rto
now	aho̲ra, ahori̲ta
the	el/ la
today	hoy
Today is Tuesday	Ho̲y es Ma̲rtes.
tomorrow	mañ̲ana
what	qué
What day is it today?	¿Qué día es ho̲y?
yesterday	aye̲r

Location

English	Spanish
here	aquí, acá
there	allí, allá, ahí

Underlined indicates the stress of the word

In parenthesis el/la indicates masculine/feminine, which normally end in "o" (if masculine) or "a" (if feminine)

Medical Vocabulary

Parts of the head

English	Spanish
head	cabeza
cheek	carrillo
chin	barbilla
ear	oreja
eye	ojo
eyebrow	ceja
eyelash	pestaña
eyelid	párpado
face	cara
forehead	(la) frente
gum	encía
hair	pelo
inner ear	oído
lip	labio
mandible	mandíbula
mouth	boca
neck	nuca
nose	(la) nariz
palate	(el) paladar
pupil	pupila
temple	(la) sien
throat	garganta
tongue	lengua
tooth	(el) diente

5. SINGULAR / PLURAL

Quick reference of the external parts of the head

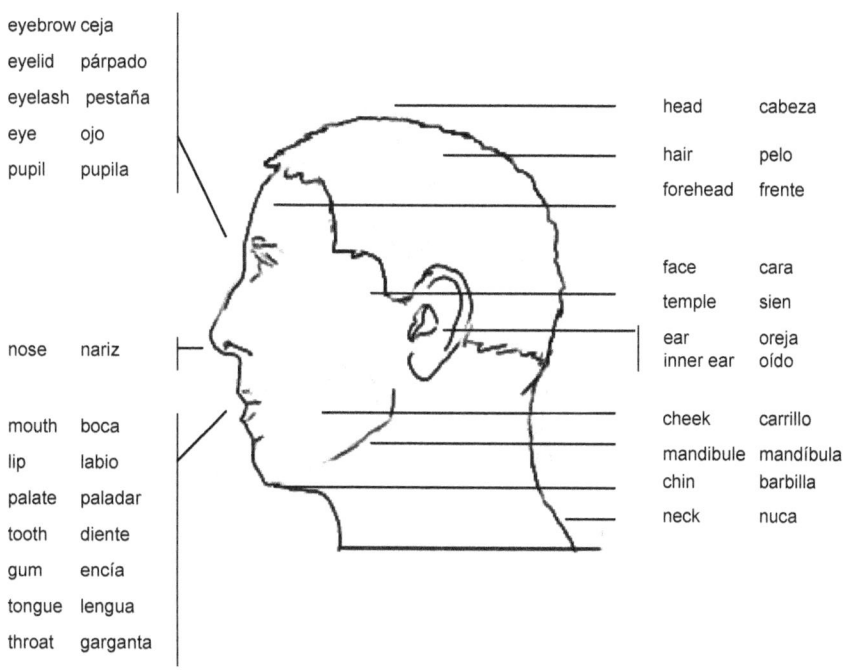

eyebrow	ceja
eyelid	párpado
eyelash	pestaña
eye	ojo
pupil	pupila
nose	nariz
mouth	boca
lip	labio
palate	paladar
tooth	diente
gum	encía
tongue	lengua
throat	garganta

head	cabeza
hair	pelo
forehead	frente
face	cara
temple	sien
ear	oreja
inner ear	oído
cheek	carrillo
mandibule	mandíbula
chin	barbilla
neck	nuca

6. MASCULINE / FEMININE
MASCULINO / FEMENINO

Some nouns have gender. In both English and Spanish, there are words that reflect this.

    boy/girl,   lion/lioness,   actor/actress
    niño/niña,   león/leona,   actor/actriz

However English nouns referring to things generally don't have gender. There are exceptions (lion/lioness). Generally, English divides the world into living and non-living things. Gender applies only to living things (he, she, man, woman, etc.). Spanish categorizes all entities into masculine and feminine.

English makes no additional distinction whether the word is masculine or feminine. Spanish does. In Spanish all words around a noun (i.e. determiners and adjectives) must have the same gender as the noun.

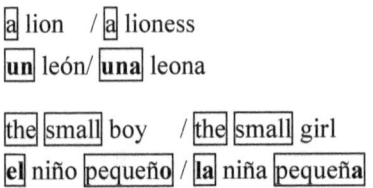

In addition, Spanish assigns a gender to **every noun**, i.e. every object, material or immaterial, can be masculine or feminine. Examples:

6. MASCULINE / FEMININE

- Masculine: cemento, kilo, carro, sonido, yate
  (= cement, kilo, car, sound, yacht)

- Feminine: guitarra, isla, hora, avenida, luz
  (= guitar, island, hour, avenue, light)

However, the words around the noun (determiners and adjectives) don't have an **intrinsic** gender. The same word can change masculine and feminine. Example: americano (= American) is an adjective, and it can be americano (masculine) or americana (feminine).

niño americano (= American boy)
niña americana (= American girl)

Rules help students recognize if a noun is masculine or feminine. These rules are based on the endings of words (meaningful endings of words are called "suffixes").

Basic Rules to Know the Gender of a Word

Golden Rule

> Words ending in an "**o**" **tend** to be masculine; words ending in an "**a**" **tend** to be feminine.

For example: el cemento, la guitarra. There are exceptions, for instance: (el) mapa, (la) mano.

Other basic rules of gender are:

- Words ending in "**-ma**" tend to be masculine, e.g. el dilema (= dilemma), el problema (= problem). There are exceptions: la calma (= calm).

- Words ending in "**-dad**," and "**-ción**" are feminine, e.g. la identidad, la diversidad, la realidad, la solución, la intervención, la atracción (= identity, diversity, reality, solution, intervention, attraction). Notice that "-dad" and "-ción" correspond to the English "-ty" and "-tion."

- Words ending in "**-ista**" ("-ist" in English) will be masculine or feminine depending on the person who is referred to, e.g. el artista (= artist) Pablo Picasso, la artista Frida Kahlo.

Besides, certain groups of nouns have a defined gender:

- The names of the letters are feminine, e.g: la A, la Be, la Ce, etc.

- The names of the numbers are masculine: el uno, el dos, el tres, etc. (= one, two, three, etc.)

- The names of countries tend to be masculine unless ending in "a." e.g. Brasil (masculine), España (feminine); "Brasil es lindo, España es linda" (= Brazil is beautiful, Spain is beautiful").

- Foreign words tend to be masculine, unless ending in "a." e.g. el software; la pizza

Collections are masculine: When you have a collection of names, with masculine **and** feminine elements in it, use the masculine gender.

I have four daughters and one son: they are my children.
Tengo cuatro hijas y un hijo: son mis hijos.

My uncles and aunts live in Texas.
Mis tíos viven en Texas.

Spain and Brazil are beautiful.
España y Brasil son lindos.

From now on, it's important that you memorize nouns with their proper gender. In Spanish dictionaries, the first information that is presented about a noun is whether it is masculine or feminine.

Warning

> Here are some basic rules that will help you. However, there are many exceptions. It is important when you learn a new word from the dictionary, you learn it with its gender (Remember: only nouns have gender).

6. MASCULINE / FEMININE

General Vocabulary

Articles and demonstratives (in natural order)

English	Spanish
a	un, una
the	el, la, los, las
this	este/ a
this thing	esto
these...	estos/as
that	ese/ a
that thing	eso
those...	esos/ as
that...over there	aquel, aquella
that thing over there	aquello
those... over there	aquellos/as
to the, at the	al (a + el)
of the	del (de + el)

Possessives (in natural order)

English	Spanish
my	mi, mis
your (singular)	tu, tus
his (as in "his house")	su, sus
her	su, sus
its	su, sus
our	nuestro/a/os/as
your (you guys) (Spain)	vuestro/a/os/as
your (you guys)	su, sus (de ustedes)
their	su, sus

Other limiting adjectives

English	Spanish
a lot	mucho
a lot of…	mucho/ a/ os/ as
a lot of…	un montón de…
all…	todo/ a/ os/ as
another	otro/ a
any, whichever	cualquiera
any…, whichever	cualquier…
both	los dos
everything	todo
little (amount)	poco
little (amount)…	poco/ a …
much	mucho / a
much	muchos/ as
no…	ningún, nunguna
none	ninguno / ninguna
none of…	ninguno/a de …
nothing	nada
other, others	otro/ a/ os /as
some	alguno / a/ os/ as
some of …	alguno / a/ os/ as de…
some…	algún / a/ os/ as
some…	unos, unas
something	algo

If you have started your vocabulary list, make sure that you write the right gender of every word on it.

In addition, the following lists are suggested to be included.

6. MASCULINE / FEMININE

The family

English	Spanish
father	(el) papá *
mother	mamá *
parents	(los) padres
son/ daughter	hijo/ a
children (sons and daughters)	hijos
brother/ sister (siblings)	hermano/ a
siblings	(los) hermanos
grandfather/ grandmother	abuelo/ a
grandparents	(los) abuelos
grandson, granddaughter	nieto/ a
grandchildren	(los) nietos
uncle/ aunt	tío/ a
nephew/ niece	sobrino/ a
cousin	primo/ a
father-in-law/ mother-in-law	suegro/ a
brother-in-law/ sister-in-law	cuñado/ a
son-in-law	yerno
daughter-in-law	nuera

(*) Formally, it's used "padre" and "madre" for father and mother. "Padre" also means "priest."

Notice that all words of the above table are nouns that have an intrinsic gender (masculine or feminine). Words of collections, as "siblings", are grammatically masculine, "los hermanos."

Genders and ages

English	Spanish
man	(el) hombre
woman	(la) mujer
boy/ girl	niño/a
adult	adulto
baby	(el) bebé
newborn	(el) recién nacido
elderly	anciano
adolescent	(el) adolescente

Medical Vocabulary

Parts of the body

English	Spanish
body	cuerpo
abdomen	(el) abdomen
ankle	tobillo
arm	brazo
armpit	axila
back	espalda
bottom	trasero
calf	pantorrilla
chest	pecho
elbow	codo
finger	dedo
foot	(el) pie
forearm	antebrazo
genitals	(los) genitales
groin	(la) ingle
hair	pelo, cabello
hand	(la) mano
head	cabeza
hip	cadera
knee	rodilla
leg	pierna
nail	uña
navel	ombligo
neck	cuello
nipple	(el) pezón
pubis	(el) pubis
shoulder	hombro
sole	planta
thigh	muslo
toe	dedo
wrist	muñeca

6. MASCULINE / FEMININE

Quick reference of the external parts of the body

hair	pelo	head	cabeza
neck	cuello	body	cuerpo
shoulder	hombro	chest	pecho
forearm	antebrazo	nipple	pezón
		armpit	axila
		back	espalda
elbow	codo	arm	brazo
wrist	muñeca	abdomen	abdomen
hand	mano	navel	omblligo
finger	dedo	hip	cadera
nail	uña	pubis	pubis
		groin	ingle
thigh	muslo	genitals	genitales
calf	pantorrilla	bottom	trasero
knee	rodilla	leg	pierna
ankle	tobillo		
foot	pie		
toe	dedo		
nail	uña		
sole	planta		

7. CONJUGATION
CONJUGACIÓN

Verbs are the nuclei of the sentence. A sentence can lack nearly anything but a verb. Verbs are all those words that describe what the subject (the person or thing) does. Examples of verbs:

    to repeat, to posses, to declare, to prefer, to toast
    repetir,   poseer,   declarar, preferir, tostar

Let's see a verb in action with other elements:

    <u>He</u>   <u>cancelled</u>   <u>his</u>   <u>ticket.</u>
    NOUN   VERB   DET.   NOUN

Every verb has many possible forms: For example, the English verb "to sing" has the variations:

    sing, sings, sang, sung, singing

We change the form of the verb depending on who is doing the action (I sing, he sings, …), and depending on when the action occurs (I sing, I sang, I will sing…).

Conjugating a verb means to put the verb in its different forms. For example, in English, the **conjugation** of the verb "to be" in the present tense is:

I am
You are
He/ She/ It is
We are
You guys are
They are

If you looked up the words "studied," "studies" or "studying" in the English dictionary you may not find them. This is because all tenses of the verb "to study" are represented only by the word "study." The form of the verb with the preposition "to" (to study) is called **the infinitive**.

Golden Rule 1

> In Spanish, the infinitive (the proxy of the verb) **always** ends with -AR, -ER or –IR.

For example:

estudi**ar**, correspond**er**, distribu**ir**
(= to study, to correspond, to distribute)

Those three endings correspond to three patterns called "conjugaciones" (= conjugations).

It's important that you learn these names:

- Verbs ending in -AR are called **AR-verbs,** or verbs of the **first conjugation.**

- Verbs ending in -ER are called **ER-verbs**, or verbs of the **second conjugation.**

- Verbs ending in -IR are called **IR-verbs**, or verbs of the **third conjugation.**

Thus, for example, you probably won't find it in the dictionary the word "estudia" (= he studies); you must look for "estudi**ar**" (= to study) which is the infinitive, the representative of its family.

The dictionary will also tell you if the verb is regular or irregular, in other words, if the verb follows the rules when it is conjugated.

English puts the information of who makes the action (I, you, he/she/it, we, you, they) before the verb (I do something). On the contrary,

Spanish puts this information **within** the verb, at the end of the verb, as a suffix.

> We adore theatre. They paint houses.
> Adoramos el teatro. Pintan casas.

Before studying those endings (as the "n" in "pintan"), you must see the translation of the pronouns: I, you, etc.

Spanish	English
yo	= I
tú	= you singular, informal
usted	= you – singular, formal
él / ella / ello	= he/ she/ it
nosotros/ nosotras	= we
vosotros/ vosotras	= you plural, only in Spain
ustedes	= you plural
ellos /ellas	= they (masculine/ feminine)

Golden Rule 2

In Spanish the subject of the sentence is always **within** the verb The translations of the English personal pronouns are suffixes: particles at the end of the verb. These are:

English	Spanish	Example
I	–VOWEL [1] or –y	plan**o**, so**y** (= **I** plan, **I** am)
you (singular informal)	–s [2]	invita**s** (= **you** invite)
you (singular formal), he/she/it	–VOWEL [1]	cuent**a** (= **he/she** counts)
We	–mos	convence**mos** (= **we** convince)
you guys (Spain)	–is	aparecé**is** (= **you** appear)
you guys, They	–n [3]	estudia**n** (= **you/ they** study)

7. CONJUGATION

(¹) These VOWELS can be: a, e, i, o, depending on the tense. For example: canto (= I sing), canté (= I sang)

(²) This is the informal "you". As explained later in this book the ending "s" has three exceptions: the past and the imperative tenses, and the verb "ser" (= to be).

(³) In Latin America the forms of "you guys" and "they" coincide. Thus, "aparece**n**" means "you guys appear" and also "they appear." The words "ustedes" (= you guys) and "ellos" (= they) are used to avoid ambiguity. See *Appendix A Notes about Dialects*.

The Personal Pronouns

Spanish does have personal pronouns such as: I, you, he, she, etc., but using them would be redundant because the information on who makes the action is already in the verb itself. So, we recommend <u>not</u> to use them unless necessary to avoid confusion.

English Pronoun	Spanish Pronoun	Spanish endings
I	yo	–VOWEL / –y
you (singular informal)	tú	–s
you (singular formal) → he/she →	usted él, ella	–VOWEL
We	nosotros	–mos
you guys (Spain)	vosotros	–is
you guys → They →	ustedes ellos	–n

Examples

yo	[yo] Estoy contento. (= I am content)
tú	[tú] Estás contento. (=You are content)
usted él, ella	[usted] Está contento. (= You are content.) [Él] Está contento. (= He is content.)
nosotros	[nosostros] Estamos contentos. (= We are content)
vosotros	[vosotros] Estáis contentos. (= You guys are content)
ustedes ellos	[ustedes] Están contentos. (= You guys are content) [ellos] Están contentos. (= They are content.)

The word in [ ] can be omitted in the sentence.

Warning: Notice that the forms of "usted" are the same as those of "él/ella". To avoid ambiguity, the words "usted" or "él/ella" are used. The same happens with the pronouns:"ustedes" and "ellos."

There is a word for "it", the pronoun "ello," but this pronoun is omitted. For example:

>It is raining.
>Está lloviendo.

The pronouns are only used to either answer "who?", to emphasize, or to avoid ambiguity.

>¿Quién responde? **Nosotros**.
>Who responds? We do.
>
>**Ella** tiene que reescribir la carta; no tú.
>She has to re-write the letter; not you.
>
>¿**Usted** está enfermo? ("Está enfermo" also means "él/ella)
>Are you sick?

Appendix A, Notes about Dialects, shows the use of the pronouns according to the three main dialects.

7. CONJUGATION

Regular Verbs

The remaining portion of the verb when we remove the AR/ER/IR part of its infinitive is called the stem. For example: the stems of:

>   admirar, responder, describir

are:

>   admir-, respond-, describ-

(as we saw in Golden Rule 1).

A verb is called regular when the corresponding endings for all persons (I, you, he, etc.) coincide with the regular endings

Let's see examples of the present tense of verbs of the three Spanish conjugations:

>   admir**ar** (= to admire) is an **AR**-verb, also called a verb of the **first** conjugation.
>   respond**er** (= to respond) is an **ER**-verb, also called a verb of the **second** conjugation.
>   describ**ir** (= to describe) is an **IR**-verb, also called a verb of the **third** conjugation.

to admire	= **admirar**
I admire	admir**o**
You admire	admir**as**
He/She/It admires	admir**a**
We admire	admir**amos**
You guys admire (Spain)	admir**áis**
You guys/ They admire	admir**an**

to respond	= **responder**
I respond	respond**o**
You respond	respond**es**
He/She/ It responds	respond**e**
We respond	respond**emos**
You guys respond	respond**éis** (Spain)
You guys/ They respond	respond**en**

to describe	= **describir**
I describe	describ**o**
You describe	describ**es**
He/She describes	describ**e**
We describe	describ**imos**
You guys describe	describ**ís** (Spain)
You guys / They describe	describ**en**

The verbs "ser" and "estar" (= to be)

You will use "estar" as "to be" when the attribute is temporary, for example:

    I am content.
    Estoy contento.

But "to be" has another translation, "ser." The verb "ser" is used when the attribute is permanent.

    I am from Peru.
    Soy de Perú.

The conjugation of these verbs are:

	ser	**estar**
(I)	s**o**y	est**o**y
(you singular)	**e**res	estás
(he/she/it)	es	está
(we)	s**o**mos	est**a**mos
(you guys)- Spain-	s**o**is	estáis
(you guys/ they)	son	están

Warning

> Certain expressions that use "to be" in English, use another verb in Spanish: "tener."

For example:

    I am hungry/ thirsty/ hot/ cold/ sleepy/ twenty years old.
    Tengo hambre/ sed/ calor/ frío/ sueño/ veinte años.

# 7. CONJUGATION

"Tener" (= to have)

"Tener" is equivalent to "to have got." So, it means to possess, or to grasp.

>I've got a house. = I posses a house.
>I've got a chair. = I grasp a chair.

It is important that you associate "tener" with "to have got", instead of simply "to have," which can be another verb in Spanish (haber). We will see in *Chapter 9 One Future, Present and Past*.

The expression "I have to" in Spanish also uses the verb "tener."
>**I've got to** cancel the appointment.
>**Tengo que** cancelar la cita.

The conjugation of *tener* is:

	tener
(I)	t<u>e</u>ngo
(you singular)	ti<u>e</u>nes
(he/she/it)	ti<u>e</u>ne
(we)	ten<u>e</u>mos
(you guys) -Spain-	tenéis
(you guys/ they)	ti<u>e</u>nen

Tips

Frequently Asked Question

FAQ: "Vosotros" or "ustedes" (= you plural)?

>"Vosotros" (= you guys) is only used in Spain. It uses the form of the second person of plural, e.g.
>
>>vosotros cantáis (= you guys sing)

"Ustedes" means "you guys" (informal) in Latinoamerica and means "you, sirs" or "you, ma'ams"(formal) in Spain. Regardless of this, "ustedes" doesn't use the forms of the second person plural, but the forms of the third person of plural, e.g.

>ustedes cantan (= you guys sing) not ~~ustedes cantáis~~

In the same way, "usted " means "you singular (and formal) in Latinoamerica, and means "you, sir" or "you, ma'am"(formal) in Spain. Regardless of this, "usted" doesn't use the forms of the second person of singular, but the forms of the third person of singular, e.g.

>usted canta (= you -singular- sing)   not ~~usted cantas~~.

This book teaches the complete range of verb forms: the six persons (all the verb tables of this book have six rows). The forms of "vosotros," i.e. the forms of the second person plural, are exceptionally regular.

The use of "usted" and "ustedes" is also explained in *Appendix A, Notes About Dialects*.

7. CONJUGATION

General Vocabulary

Personal pronouns

English	Spanish
I	yo
you – singular, informal	tú
you – singular, formal	usted
he/ she/ it	él / ella / *
we	nosotros/ as
you – plural (Spain)	vosotros/ as
you – plural	ustedes
they	ellos /as

(*) The word "it" as in "It is my house" is not translated in Spanish: "Es mi casa."

The verbs for "to be" (= ser/ estar)

The verb "to be" use two verbs: *ser* and *estar* in Spanish. *Ser* is used for permanent attributes; *estar* for non-permanent attributes. Example:

Martin **is** from the Unites States. Martin **is** in Italy now.
Martín **es** de los Estados Unidos. Martin **está** en Italia ahora.

The following is the conjugation for the present tense of the verbs "ser" and "estar."

English	Spanish	
to be	ser	estar
I am	soy	estoy
You (singular) are	eres	estás
He/ She/ It is	es	está
We are	somos	estamos
You guys are (Spain)	sois	estáis
You guys/ They are	son	están

Remember that the underscore mark is just a hint in this book to tell you where the stressed vowel is, and to make it easier to learn the words with their correct pronunciation.

The verbs for "to have" (= tener/ haber)

English	Spanish
to have	ten_e_r
I have	t_e_ngo
You have	ti_e_nes
He/ She/ It has	ti_e_ne
We have	ten_e_mos
You guys have (Spain)	tenéis
You guys/ They have	ti_e_nen

Sample of descriptive adjectives that use "ser"

English	Spanish
American (from the US)	americ_a_no/ a
Cuban	cub_a_no/ a
Dominican	dominic_a_no/ a
Mexican	mejic_a_no/ a, mexic_a_no/ a
Puerto Rican	puertorriqu_e_ño/ a

Sample of descriptive adjectives that use "estar"

English	Spanish
alive	v_i_vo
asleep	dorm_i_do
dead	mu_e_rto
healthy	s_a_no
nervous	nervi_o_so
sick	enf_e_rmo
tired	cans_a_do
worried	preocup_a_do
wounded	her_i_do

7. CONJUGATION

Medical Vocabulary

Organs

English	Spanish
organ	órgano
anus	ano
appendix	(el) apéndice
bladder	vejiga
brain	cerebro
bronchi	bronquio
colon	(el) colon
diaphragm	(el) diafragma
esophagus	esófago
gallbladder	vesícula
heart	(el) corazón
intestine	intestino
kidney	(el) riñón
large intestine	intestino grueso
larynx	(la) laringe
liver	hígado
lung	(el) pulmón
ovary	ovario
pancreas	(el) páncreas
penis	(el) pene
pharynx	(la) faringe
placenta	placenta
prostate	próstata
rectum	recto
small intestine	intestino delgado
sphincter	(el) esfínter
spinal cord	espina dorsal
spleen	bazo
stomach	estómago
testicle	testículo
trachea	tráquea
uterus	útero
vagina	vagina

8. HOW TO LEARN WORDS EFFICIENTLY
CÓMO APRENDER PALABRAS EFICIENTEMENTE

As we saw in the last three chapters, when you look up a word in the dictionary, you must look for the proxy of that word. Examples:

"carro" (singular), not "carros" (plural)
"gato" (masculine), not "gata" (feminine)
"estudi**ar**" (infinitive), not "estudi**é**" (= to study, not studied)

The proxy must be singular and masculine (if the word is a noun, determiner or adjective) and infinitive (if the word is a verb).

As for the meaning, we can classify words in two main categories:

Non-grammatical words are those words with an actual meaning by itself: dog, white, walking, Peter, fast, attitude,...These are the words that you can describe when you play the party game charades.

Grammatical words are those words that create the structure of the sentence: the, a, at, to, over, however, maybe, on, another, by...

You could only communicate very primitively without grammatical words. Grammatical words form the structure of the sentence. For example, in the sentence "Your cat is on the table," if you removed the grammatical words the result would be absurd:

(Your) cat is (on the) table → cat is table

8. HOW TO LEARN WORDS EFFICIENTLY

Regarding the non-grammatical words: you will have to choose which of these words you want to learn every day according to your areas of specialty: emergency, cardiology, etc. There's a reason for this: The words that you pick yourself will be the ones that you will enjoy memorizing, and the ones that you will end up utilizing. This book will give you recommendations and clues to look up non-grammatical words in the dictionary.

Regarding the grammatical words, *Chapter 11 Grammar Rules*, will go over these words extensively. Some will be explained in the body of each chapter, others will appear in the vocabulary section of each chapter.

We recommend the following method. Take it as a **golden rule.**

> - **Learn a consistent number of words a day** (say ten). Flash cards are a great idea to test yourself; in turn, using a computer spreadsheet for those words is the best way to keep a record. It enables you to sort your learned words and keep them organized.
>
> - **Pick your own words**. Select the grammatical words from this book, and the non-grammatical words from your areas of interest. Lists or families of words work better than unlinked words. For example, if you are keen on painting, learn the list of basic colors as part of your daily set of words (vs., one color and nine other words today, and another color with another nine words tomorrow).
>
> - **Notice if the words you are picking have similarities with English in any form**. Being aware of the commonalities will help you not only memorize the word but also memorize other words of its family.

Cognates, Indirect Cognates and False Cognates

A distinction can be made regarding the similar words in both languages. On one hand, there are "**cognates**," those words from Spanish that are easy to translate and recognize, for instance teléfono/telephone or artista/artist.

On the other hand, there is what we can call "**indirect cognates**," those words whose similarities are not evident, but are based on other words of the same family. For instance, "agua" is not a cognate of "water;" however, you can find the meaning through the cognate: aquarium/acuario.

There are hundreds of cognates, and hundreds of indirect cognates. Below you will find a list of indirect cognates:

English	Spanish	Cognate English/Spanish
big	grande	grand = gran
body	cuerpo	corporal = corporal
bone	hueso	osteoporosis = osteoporosis
brain	cerebro	cerebral = cerebral
dead	muerto	morgue = morgue
eye	ojo	ocular = ocular
hand	mano	manual = manual
heart	corazón	cardiogram = cardiograma
hundred	cien	cent = céntimo
kidney	riñón	renal = renal
lung	pulmón	pulmonary = pulmonar
man	hombre	human = humano
meat	carne	carnivore = carnívoro
milk	leche	lactose = lactosa
month	mes	semester = semestre
moon	luna	lunar = lunar
mouth	boca	bucal = bucal
one	uno	unit = unidad
skin	piel	to peel = pelar
sun	sol	solar = solar
thousand	mil	mile = milla
to be born	nacer	native = nativo
to drink	beber	beverage = bebida
to feel	sentir	sentiment = sentimiento
to live	vivir	to survive = sobrevivir
to see	ver	visible = visible
to sleep	dormir	dormant = durmiente
tongue	lengua	language = lenguaje
tooth	diente	dentist = dentista
water	agua	aquarium = acuario
year	año	annual = anual

8. HOW TO LEARN WORDS EFFICIENTLY

A **false cognate** is a word that resembles another in the another language but has a different meaning. For example "constipated" sounds like "constipado," but the latter means "sick with a cold." Examples:

English	Spanish
constipated	estreñido
sick with a cold	constipado

English	Spanish
preservative	conservante
condom	preservativo, condón

English	Spanish
actual	real
current, today's	actual

Spanglish

Spanglish is what results when you insert English words (genuine or altered) in a Spanish speech or viceversa.

> Si tomo la **freeway**, llego allí antes.

This means: "If I take the freeway, I get there sooner;" where "freeway" is not a Spanish word.

In some cases, as the one above, the word is genuine: it has been taken from English as is (in spelling and pronunciation): La freeway, el bill, los taxes, el VCR, el U-turn, el e-mail, or el zip code. Other times, the word is altered: it has suffered some adaptation to the Spanish pronunciation:

> la troca (= truck), la marketa (= market), la yarda (= yard), las utilidades (= utilities), las partes (= auto-parts), lonchear (= to have lunch), parkear (= to park), likear (= to leak)

Occasionally, the newborn word can conflict with another word existing in the Spanish standard:

Non-standard Spanish	Standard Spanish
carpeta (= carpet)	carpeta (= folder)
remover (= to remove)	remover (= to stir)
ordenar (= to order food)	ordenar (= to command)

Prefixes and Suffixes

A prefix is an initial particle of a word with meaning. It is called suffix if it goes at the end of the word. For example the prefix "un" means "opposite." Thus, for example: "unnecessary" means "not necessary."

The vast majority of prefixes and suffixes are the same or very similar in both Spanish and English. Below, you will find just a sample:

English		Spanish	
-al	e.g. renal	-al	e.g. renal
-algia	e.g. neuralgia	-algia	e.g. neuralgia
-ism	e.g. astigmatism	-ismo	e.g. astigmatismo
-ist	e.g. dentist	-ista	e.g. dentista
-itis	e.g. meningitis	-itis	e.g. meningitis
-osis	e.g. thrombosis	-osis	e.g. trombosis
-tion	e.g. preparation	-ción	e.g. preparación
-ty	e.g. integrity	-dad	e.g. integridad
anti-	e.g. antihistame	anti-	e.g. antihistamínico
extra-	e.g. extraordinary	ex-	e.g. extraordinario
post-	e.g. post operation	post-	e.g. postoperación
pre-	e.g. prenatal	pre-	e.g. prenatal
un-	e.g. unnecessary	in-	e.g. innecesario

Tips

Frequently Asked Question

FAQ: Where do I find the "grammatical words" that I have to learn?

> In the General Vocabulary at the end of each chapter, you will find relevant grammatical words related with the chapter. These words are included also in the *Index of Grammatical Words* at the end of the book..

8. HOW TO LEARN WORDS EFFICIENTLY

General Vocabulary

Remember "tener" (to have got)
(seen in *Chapter 7 Conjugation*).

English	Spanish
to have got	tener
I have got	tengo
you (singular) have got	tienes
he/she/it has got	tiene
we have got	tenemos
you guys have got -Spain-	tenéis
you guys/ they have got	tienen

The verb "hacer" (= to make)

English	Spanish
to make	hacer
I make	hago
you (singular) make	haces
he/she/it makes	hace
we make	hacemos
you guys- Spain- make	hacéis
you guys/ they make	hacen

Nouns that go with "tener" (= to have got)
unlike English, which go with "to be" (= ser/ estar)

English	Spanish
hunger (e.g. I am hungry.)	(el) hambre (e.g. tengo hambre.)
thirsty	(la) sed
sleepy	sueño
60 years old	60 años
hot	(el) calor
cold	frío
scared	miedo

Nouns that go with "hacer" (= to make)
unlike English, which go with "to be" (= ser/ estar)

English	Spanish
wind (e.g. It's windy)	vi̱ento (e.g. Hace viento *)
sunny	(el) sol
good wheather	bu̱en ti̱empo
bad wheather	mal ti̱empo
cold	frío **
hot	(el) caḻor

(*) Notice that "hace" literally means "it makes" according to the table of the verb "hacer."

(**) Also notice that "hacer" will be used when the sentence is impersonal, e.g. "**Hace** frío" (= It's cold); unlike tener, which is used when the sentence is personal, e.g. "**Tengo** frío" (I am cold).

Spanglish

Some Spanish words are **only** found in the US. They are adaptations of Latin root words in the English language. They do not belong to the standard Spanish; however, they are very common in the U.S.

Some of the most popular ones are:

English	Spanglish	Spanish
application	(la) aplicación	(la) soliciṯud
form	f̱orma	formuḻario
carpet	carp̱eta	alf̱ombra
truck	tṟoca	camioṉeta
eligibility	elegibiliḏad	(los) deṟechos
rent	ṟenta	(el) alquiḻer
backyard	y̱arda	p̱atio
utilities	utiliḏades	serv̱icios de gas, etc.
auto-part	(la) p̱arte	pi̱eza

Medical Vocabulary

Bones

English	Spanish
bones	**huesos**
carpus	c<u>a</u>rpo
clavicle	clavícula
falange	(la) fal<u>a</u>nge
femur	(el) fémur
fibula	(el) peroné
hip	cad<u>e</u>ra
humerus	húmero
mandible	mandíbula
metacarpus	metac<u>a</u>rpo
metatarsus	metat<u>a</u>rso
patella	rótula
pelvis	(la) p<u>e</u>lvis
radial	r<u>a</u>dio
rib	cost<u>i</u>lla
scapula	omóplato
skull	cráneo
spine	(la) col<u>u</u>mna vertebr<u>a</u>l
sternum	(el) esternón
tarsus	t<u>a</u>rso
tibia	t<u>i</u>bia
ulna	cúbito
vertebra	vértebra

SECTION III

SENTENCES
ORACIONES

Remember, from today on, it is recommended that you learn a number of words a day. Your daily set of words should be divided into two categories. One category is grammatical words. You will find many of them at the end of every chapter (General Vocabulary). For the other category, the non-grammatical words, you can pick them on your own depending on your areas of interest (examen, virus, pulmón, etc.). Learn these words in groups (bones, organs, procedures, etc.).

Verbs are the essential part of sentences (you can't have a sentence without a verb). In the chapters 9 and 10, you will learn more about verbs.

You will learn about the different types of words (nouns, adjectives, verbs, etc.) in *Chapter 11 Grammar Rules.*

In the last chapter of this section, you will learn how to convert statements into questions and negative sentences.

When you finish Section III, you will be able to build your own sentences.

9. ONE FUTURE, PRESENT, AND PAST
UN FUTURO, PRESENTE Y PASADO

To start building sentences in the present, past, and future, we can use the three simplest Verb Structures: "I am singing, I am going to sing, I have sung." They are the simplest because there are few or no irregular verbs in these forms. The examples of this book use these three structures extensively.

These are the constructions to study:

        I am going to sing [future]   "Voy a cant**ar**"
        I am singing [present]   "Estoy cant**ando**"
        I have sung [past]   "He cant**ado**"

Where:

        The form "to sing" is called the "infinitive" of the verb "to sing"
        The form "sing" is called the "gerund" of the verb "to sing"
        The form "sung" is called the "participle" of the verb "to sing"

Every conjugation (AR, ER, IR) has its own set of **endings**. In bold we have marked the endings that correspond to verbs for the three conjugations.

9. ONE FUTURE, PRESENT, AND PAST

AR Verbs	ER Verbs	IR Verbs
-ar e.g cantar (= to sing)	-er e.g beber (= to drink)	-ir e.g vivir (= to live)
-ando e.g. cantando (= singing)	-iendo e.g bebiendo (= drinking)	-iendo e.g viviendo (= living)
-ado e.g. cantado (= sung)	-ido e.g bebido (= drunk)	-ido e.g vivido (= lived)

These three tenses (I am going to sing, I'm singing, , and I have sung) use three auxiliary verbs, which are: to be (estar), to go (ir) and to have (haber). In order to use these tenses appropriately you need to know the present tense of those three verbs.

One Future: "I am going to sing"

The structure "I am going to sing" uses the verb "ir" (=to go) conjugated, in other words, the verb "ir" changes with the persons I, you, he, etc.

Ir = to go

English	Spanish
I go	voy
you singular go	vas
he/she/it goes	va
we go	vamos
you guys go	vais (Spain)
you guys/ they go	van

Thus, I am going to sing, you are going to sing, etc. will be:

English		Spanish	
I am going	to sing	Voy	a cantar
You are going	to sing	Vas	a cantar
He/she is going	to sing	Va	a cantar
We are going	to sing	Vamos a cantar	
You guys are going	to sing	Vais	a cantar (Spain)
You guys/They are going	to sing	Van	a cantar

Notice that the translation doesn't occur word for word: "*Voy a cantar*" is literally "I go to sing," but the translation is "I am going to sing."

Other examples:

I am going to establish a record.
Voy a establec**er** un récord.

They are going to divide the property.
Van a divid**ir** la propiedad.

One Present "I am singing"

The structure "I am singing" uses the verb "estar" (= to be) conjugated, in other words, the verb "estar" changes with the persons I, you, he, etc.

Estar = to be

English	Spanish
I am	est<u>o</u>y
You singular are	estás
He/she/it is	está
We are	est<u>a</u>mos
You guys are (Spain)	estáis
You guys are/ they are	están

9. ONE FUTURE, PRESENT, AND PAST

Thus, I am singing, You are singing, etc. will be:

English		Spanish	
I am	singing	Estoy	cantando
You are	singing	Estás	cantando
He is /she is	singing	Está	cantando
We are	singing	Estamos	cantando
You guys are	singing	Estáis	cantando (Spain)
You guys/ They are	singing	Están	cantando

Unlike the structure we had before ("I am going to sing"), this is a literal translation: I am = *estoy*; singing = *cantando*.

Other examples:

I am establishing a record.
Estoy estable**iendo** un récord.

They are dividing the property.
Están divid**iendo** la propiedad.

One Past "I have sung"

The structure "I have sung" uses the verb "haber" (= to be) conjugated, in other words, the verb "haber" changes with the persons I, you, he, etc.

Haber = to have (auxiliary)

English	Spanish
I have (e.g. I have studied.)	he (e.g. He estudiado.)
You singular have	has
He/she/it has	ha
We have	hemos
You guys have (Spain)	habéis
You guys / They have	han

Thus, "I have sung," "you have sung," etc. will be:

English		Spanish
I have	sung	He cantado
You have	sung	Has cantado
He/she has	sung	Ha cantado
We have	sung	Hemos cantado
You guys have	sung	Habéis cantado (Spain)
You guys/ They have	sung	Han cantado

This structure is a literal translation: I have = *he*; sung = *cantado*.

Other examples:

I have established a record.
He estable**cido** un récord.

They have divided the property.
Han divid**ido** la propiedad

Tips

Frequently Asked Questions

FAQ 1: Are there any verbs that don't follow the rules to construct the present, the past, or the future?

Few. In fact, the great advantages of learning these three tenses are the ease to memorize and the low number of irregular verbs in these tenses.

For example the verb "poner" (= to put) is irregular in the past tense. Thus, we write "puesto" instead of ~~ponido.~~

I have put the termometer there.
He puesto el termómetro allí.

This will be the topic of next chapter, *Chapter 10 Irregularities in the Future, Present and Past*.

9. ONE FUTURE, PRESENT, AND PAST

FAQ 2: In English the forms "to sing", "singing," and "sung" can function as something different than a verb (an action). Is it the same in Spanish?

Yes, it is. Let's see this with some examples on the verb to drink and its forms: drinking and drunk.

Drinking is a problem.
(Here the verb is "is" –to be. "Singing" functions as a noun. What is my passion? Singing).

You are not going to solve your problems by **drinking**.
(Here the verb is "to solve." The word "drinking" functions as an adverb. **How** you are not going to solve your problems? Drinking).

He is **drunk**.
(Here the verb is "is" –to be. "drunk functions as an adjective. What is his attribute or condition? drunk).

Spanish is the same, with the exception of the first case. In the first case, Spanish uses the infinitive ("to drink", instead of "drinking").

Beber es un problema.
No vas a solucionar tus problemas **bebiendo**.
Está **bebido**.

Other examples:

Acting in front of a large audience is my dream.
Actuar en frente de una gran audiencia es mi sueño.

I'm educating my voice by singing in the shower.
Estoy educando mi voz cantando en la ducha.

Are not you guys altering the document by eliminating the appendices?
¿No están (estáis –Spain-) alterando el documento al eliminar los apéndices?

General Vocabulary

The verb "ir" (= to go)

English	Spanish
to go	ir
I go	voy
you (singular) go	vas
he/she/it goes	va
we go	vamos
you guys go -Spain-	vais
you guys/ they go	van

Remember "estar," (= to be -temporal, *Chapter 7 Conjugation*)

English	Spanish
to be	estar
I am	estoy
You (singular) are	estás
He/ She/ It is	está
We are	estamos
You guys are -Spain-	estáis
You guys/ They are	están

The verb "haber" (= to have, as an auxiliary verb)

English	Spanish
to have (auxiliary)	haber
I have (e.g. I have studied.)	he (e.g. He estudiado.)
you (singular) have	has
he/she/it has	ha
we have	hemos
you guys have -Spain-	habéis
you guys/ they have	han

The only grammatical words among the verbs are the auxiliary verbs: to have (haber), to be (ser and estar), and to go (ir). When they act as auxiliary verbs they are a structural part of a sentence.

Medical Vocabulary

Fluids, vessels, glands, and tissues

English	Spanish
fluid	fluido
vessel	vaso
gland	glándula
tissue	tejido
amniotic liquid	líquido amniótico
artery	arteria
bile	(la) bilis
blood	(la) sangre
blood vessel	vaso sanguíneo
bone	hueso
capillary	(el) capilar
cartilage	cartílago
earwax	(el) cerumen
feces, poop	(las) heces, caca
gastric acid	jugo gástrico
hormone	hormona
ligament	ligamento
lymphatic node	nódulo linfático
lymphatic vessel	vaso linfático
mammary gland	glándula mamaria
mucosa	mucosa
mucus, snot	moco
muscle	músculo
nerve	nervio
phlegm	flema
saliva	saliva
semen	(el) semen
skin	(la) piel
sweat	(el) sudor
tear	lágrima
tendons	(el) tendón
thyroid	(la) tiroides
ureters	(el) uréter
urethra	uretra
urine, piss	orina, (el) pis
vein	vena

10. IRREGULARITIES IN FUTURE, PRESENT, AND PAST
IRREGULARIDADES EN EL FUTURO, PRESENTE Y PASADO

Let's remember the endings:

AR Verbs	ER Verbs	IR Verbs
-**ar** e.g cantar (= to sing)	-**er** e.g beber (= to drink)	-**ir** e.g vivir (= to live)
-**ando** e.g. cantando (= singing)	-**iendo** e.g bebiendo (= drinking)	-**iendo** e.g viviendo (= living)
-**ado** e.g. cantado (= sung)	-**ido** e.g bebido (= drunk)	-**ido** e.g vivido (= lived)

Also remember:

       The form in AR, ER, IR is called **infinitive**.
       The form in ANDO, IENDO is called **gerund**.
       The form in ADO, IDO is called **participle** (or past participle)

A verb is irregular in the infinitive, gerund or participle (in other words: future, present or past) if it doesn't have the exact ending corresponding to future, present and past.

10. IRREGULARITIES IN FUTURE, PRESENT, AND PAST

Thus, for example, the verb "morir" (= to die) is irregular in both the gerund and participle form, which are: "muriendo" and "**muerto**." By checking the table before, you see that the verb doesn't follow the rule:

IR verbs	if regular, it would be:	instead, it is:
-ir		morir (= to die)
-iendo	mor iendo	muriendo (= dying)
-ido	mor ido	muerto (= died)

Irregular Verbs in the Infinitive (to sing)

Let's remember the golden rule of *Chapter 7 Conjugation*:

> **All** verbs have their infinitive ending in AR, ER or IR. (The stem of the verb is what is left when you take out the ending AR, ER, or IR from its infinitive).

Thus, there is no irregular verb in the infinitive form.

Irregular Verbs in the Gerund (singing)

An example of an irregular verb in the gerund is "atribuir" (= to attribute). Its gerund is not ~~atribuiendo,~~ but atribuyendo.

There are four types of irregularities:

Type 1. Affects all verbs ending with -aer, -eer, -oer, -oír, -uir. e.g. atribuir.

These verbs insert a "y" between the stem and the ending, (otherwise it would sound strange with three vowels together)
e.g. atribu-ir → atribuiendo → atribuyendo (= attributing).

Infinitive		Gerund
atribuir	= to attribute	atribuyendo
caer	= to fall	cayendo
construir	= to construct	construyendo
contribuir	= to contribute	contribuyendo
creer	= to believe	creyendo
destruir	= to destruct	destruyendo
distribuir	= to distribute	distribuyendo
huir	= to flee	huyendo
incluir	= to include	incluyendo
leer	= to reed	leyendo
oír	= to hear	oyendo
poseer	= to posses	poseyendo
proveer	= to supply	proveyendo
traer	= to bring	trayendo

Type 2. Affects two verbs. Those IR verbs whose infinitive have an –o- in the second to last syllable.

These verbs change o → u, in order to form the gerund.

dor-mir → durmiendo (= sleeping)

Infinitive		Gerund
dormir	= to sleep	durmiendo
morir	= to die	muriendo

Type 3. Affects all verbs of the third conjugation (IR verbs) whose infinitive have an -e- in the second to last syllable.

These verbs change e → i to form their gerund.

      a-rre-pen-tir → arrepintiendo (= repenting)

10. IRREGULARITIES IN FUTURE, PRESENT, AND PAST 101

Examples:

Infinitive		Gerund
arrepentir	= to repent	arrepintiendo
conseguir	= to achieve	consiguiendo
convertir	= to convert	convirtiendo
corregir	= to correct	corrigiendo
decir	= to say	diciendo
despedir	= to see so. off./ to fire	despidiendo
divertir	= to have fun	divirtiendo
elegir	= to choose	eligiendo
freír	= to fry	friendo
gemir	= to wine	gimiendo
herir	= to cause a wound	hiriendo
hervir	= to boil	hirviendo
inferir	= to infer	infiriendo
invertir	= to invert	invirtiendo
medir	= to measure	midiendo
mentir	= to lie	mintiendo
pedir	= to ask for	pidiendo
preferir	= to prefer	prefiriendo
reír	= to laugh	riendo
rendir	= to surrender	rindiendo
reñir	= to quarrel	riñiendo
repetir	= to repeat	repitiendo
seguir	= to go on	siguiendo
sentir	= to feel	sintiendo
servir	= to serve	sirviendo
sonreír	= to smile	sonriendo
sugerir	= to suggest	sugiriendo
venir	= to come	viniendo
vestir	= to dress	vistiendo

You will also see similar irregularities in the present tense (*Chapter 16 The Present and Past Tense*s).

Type 4. Others.

There are only two verbs that don't conform to any rule for their irregularity. These are:

Infinitive		Gerund
ir	= to go	yendo
poder	= can	pudiendo

Irregular Verbs in the Past Participle (Sung)

There are only 13 common verbs with an irregular participle. For example, for "abrir" (= to open), it is "abierto," not ~~abrido~~.

Below you'll find the list of verbs that are irregular in the Past Participle.

Infinitive		Past Participle
abrir	= to open	abierto
cubrir	= to cover	cubierto
escribir	= to write	escrito
decir	= to say	dicho
hacer	= to do	hecho
morir	= to die	muerto
poner	= to put	puesto
resolver	= to resolve	resuelto
romper	= to break	roto
satisfacer	= to satisfy	satisfecho
soltar	= to loosen up	suelto
volver	= to come back	vuelto
ver	= to see	visto

Tips

Frequently Asked Questions

FAQ: Are "died" and "dead" the same word in Spanish?

> Yes, they are: "muerto." Consider the English word "tired." It's the same for: "I am **tired**", and "I have **tired** him by running."

10. IRREGULARITIES IN FUTURE, PRESENT, AND PAST

General Vocabulary

There are two types of words whose function is to join: the prepositions, which links parts of the sentence, and the conjunction, which joins one clause with another.

Preposiones

English	Spanish
about	sobre
according to	según
after	tras (*Voy tras él.* = *I go after him.*)
against	contra
around	alrededor de
at	a, en (*)
at, in, on	en, sobre (*)
at/ in the beginning of...	al principio de
at/ in the end of...	al final de
between, among	entre
by	para, por (*)
far from	lejos de
for	para, por (*)
in the middle of...	en medio de
inside...	dentro de
near, close to, around...	cerca de
next to...	junto a
of, from, off	de, desde (*)
on top of...	encima de
outside...	fuera de
side by side...	al lado de
to	para, a (*)
to, towards	hacia
under	bajo (*Está bajo la cama* = *It's under the bed*)
underneath	debajo de / abajo de (same as above)
until, up to	hasta
with	con
without	sin

(*) Translation varies depending on the context

Conjunctions

English	Spanish
although	aunque
and	y
as	a medida que
as	como
as per	en cuanto a…
as soon as	tan pronto como
because	porque
because of	por
because of	por causa de
but	pero
but	sino
due to	debido a
either…or…	o…o..
given that	dado que
however	sin embargo
if	si
I mean	o sea
in case that	en el caso de que
in other words	en otras palabras
in spite of	a pesar de
in view that	en vista de que/ visto que
like	al igual que
like	como
neither …nor…	ni…ni…
nevertheless	no obstante
or	o
since	puesto que/ ya que
so that	para que
then, afterwards	entonces
then, afterwards	luego
under the condition that	a condición de que
unless	a menos que
unlike	a diferencia de
while, as long as	mientras

Medical Vocabulary

Elements, chemicals, and nutrients

English	Spanish
element	elem<u>e</u>nto
chemical	prod<u>u</u>cto químico
nutrient	(el) nutri<u>e</u>nte
acid	ácido
air	(el) <u>a</u>ire
base	(la) b<u>a</u>se
calcium	c<u>a</u>lcio
carbohydrate	carbohidr<u>a</u>to
chlorine	cl<u>o</u>ro
CO	monóxido de carb<u>o</u>no
CO2	dióxido de carb<u>o</u>no
fat	gr<u>a</u>sa
fluoride	fluor<u>u</u>ro
fluorine	(el) flúor
gas	(el) gas
glucose	gluc<u>o</u>sa
glycerine	glicer<u>i</u>na
hydrogen	hidrógeno
ice	hi<u>e</u>lo
iodine	y<u>o</u>do
iron	hi<u>e</u>rro
liquid	líquido
mercury	merc<u>u</u>rio
metal	(el) met<u>a</u>l
mineral	(el) miner<u>a</u>l
nitrogen	nitrógeno
oxygen	oxígeno
potassium	pot<u>a</u>sio
protein	proteína
salt	(la) sal
sodium	s<u>o</u>dio
solid	sólido
sulphur	(el) az<u>u</u>fre
vitamin A, B, etc.	vitam<u>i</u>na A, B, etc.
water	(el) <u>a</u>gua
water steam	(el) vap<u>o</u>r de <u>a</u>gua

11. GRAMMAR RULES
REGLAS GRAMATICALES

Words can be divided into many ways but for the purpose of learning effectively (fast), two main classifications arise. On one hand, words can be classified into nine types according to their functionality in a sentence (nouns, adjectives, verbs, etc.). On the other hand, overlapping this classification, words can also be classified into two main groups (grammatical and non grammatical words), depending on their having either a structural value or a concrete meaning.

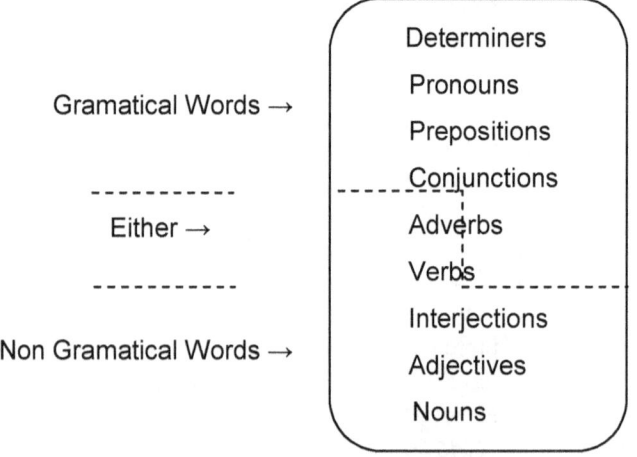

The grammatical words are those words that you need to build a sentence but that don't have a concrete meaning, for example:

    in, or, other, not, my
    en, o, otro, no, mi

11. GRAMMAR RULES

Conversely, **the non grammatical words** are those for which you can come out with a definition easily, for example:

    car, gray, studying, rapidly
    carro, gris, estudiando, rápidamente

The importance of learning this categorization is to help you in the learning process and distinguish those words that have a structural importance (grammatical) from those that are "just vocabulary" (non grammatical). This book includes an extensive list of grammatical words for easy consultation, *Index of Grammatical Words*.

As per the other classification, words can be:

- **Interjections** (interjecciones): Hello! Bye!
- **Determiners** (determinantes): the, a, an, five, these...
- **Adjectives** (adjetivos): green, large, true, productive...
- **Nouns** (nombres): Peter, house, truth, productivity...
- **Pronouns** (pronombres): we, us, ours, ourselves, me...
- **Adverbs** (adverbios) rapidly, quietly, strongly...
- **Prepositions** (preposiciones): of, for, at, on, in, under...
- **Conjunctions** (conjunciones): and, or, yet, but, what, if...
- **Verbs** (verbos): am, have, goes, worked, eaten...

Let's see one example in one sentence:

<u>Wow! That gray dog that she bought in Germany runs fast!</u>
INTERJ. DET. ADJ. NOUN CONJ PRON. VERB PREP. NOUN VERB ADVERB

Each of these nine types identifies one function, but one same word can have different roles in different sentences. In the following example, the word "milk" has different uses (i.e. it functions as different types)

    Noun: **Milk** is the product from cows.
    Adjective   **Milk** products sell well.
    Verb: The farmers **milk** the cows everyday.

Grammatical words are: determiners, pronouns, prepositions, conjunctions, a few adverbs, and the auxiliary verbs (to have, to be and to go). **Non-grammatical words** are: interjections, nouns, adjectives, most adverbs and verbs.

The following table displays the most important features of each type of words.

Type	Grammatical Words?	Masculine / femenine	Singular / plural	Person & tense
Interjections	no	no	no	no
Determiners	yes	yes	yes	no
Adjectives	no	yes	yes	no
Nouns	no	yes **	yes	no
Pronouns	yes	yes	yes	no
Adverbs	a few *	no	no	no
Prepositions	yes	no	no	no
Conjunctions	yes	no	no	no
Verbs	a few *	no	no	yes

(*) Because of their grammatical value we can consider grammatical words adverbs like "muy" (= very), "aquí" (= here), and the four auxiliary verbs: "ser," "estar" (both meaning "to be"), haber (= to have) and "ir" (= to go).

(**) Nouns have an intrinsic gender. They have a fixed gender: either masculine or feminine. Other types, for example determiners, have both.

As explained in the previous chapter, words can be classified into types (nouns, verbs, etc.) as per their function in the sentence. All types have their own rules.

The following are the definitions and elementary rules of the nine types of words.

Interjections

Interjections are those expressive words that constitute a sentence by themselves: Wow, Ah, Ouch, OK, Bye, etc. They are invariable.

Golden Rule

> Interjections make up sentences by themselves, and they are invariable. They don't change regardless of occurring in the past, present or future, or for having one subject or another. As a consequence, each interjection is to be learned as is, with no further analysis.

For example, the English expression "Wow!" means "I am surprised by that," regardless of the context being in the present, past or future; regardless of who speaks (one or more people, masculine or feminine, etc.). Conversely, the equivalent sentence "I am surprised by that" is formed by pieces (each word) that are subject to grammar rules to be combined and have different meanings: "I was surprised by that," "He is surprised by that…"

Determiners

The determiners are those words that complement the noun, as: the, a, some, this, our… In Spanish, unlike the adjectives (which also qualify the noun), determiners go before the noun.

>   The difficult lesson
>   DET. ADJ.   NOUN

>   La lección difícil
>   DET. ADJ. NOUN

Golden Rule

> All determiners go before the noun, and they correspond to the noun in number (singular/plural) and in gender (masculine/feminine).

For example, the translation of the English THE is the following:

>   the boy/ the girl / the boys /the girls
>   **el** niño /**la** niña/ **los** niños / **las** niñas

Adjectives

The adjectives are the words that inform us about qualities of the noun e.g. blue, large, expensive, happy, etc. Words like "tired" function as adjectives, although derived from verbs ("to tire").

Golden Rule

> Adjectives correspond with the noun in number (singular/plural) and in gender (masculine/feminine). They go after the noun, with some exceptions.

Unlike English, Spanish adjectives must correspond with their noun in number and gender. Example, "automático:"

>an automatic watch; some automatic watches
>un reloj automáti**co**, unos relojes automáti**cos**

>an automatic machine; some automatic machines
>una máquina automáti**ca**, unas máquinas automáti**cas**

The exceptions are: "buen" (= good) "mal"(= bad), "primer" (= first), "tercer" (= third), and "gran" (=great).

Unlike English, Spanish can't create adjectives out of nouns. For example, "kidney" is a noun, but in the expression "kidney failure," it functions as a adjective.

Spanish can do something similar by using "de" (= of):

>**kidney** failure
>fallo del **riñón**

In addition, English and Spanish can also use the corrresponding adjective:

>renal failure
>fallo renal

Nouns

Nouns are all words that represent entities, such as persons, animals, plants, objects, places or ideas. For example: Jose, woman, zebra, pear, California, milk, love, velocity.

Golden Rule

> All nouns in Spanish have an intrinsic gender regardless of whether or not they denote persons, animals or objects. (Words ending in "o" are more likely to be masculine; ending in "a", feminine). In addition, when we refer to more than one element, nouns add an "s" (or "es" if the word doesn't end in: a, e, i, o, u).

11. GRAMMAR RULES

Examples:

    José [masc.], mujer [fem.], cebra [fem.], pera [fem.], California [fem.], leche [fem.], amor [masc.], velocidad [fem.]

    (= Jose, woman, zebra, pear, California, milk, love, velocity)

    un carro, dos carros, un computador, dos computadores
    one car, two cars, one computer, two computers

Pronouns

Pronouns are those words that substitute for a noun. Thanks to them, when the subject of the sentence is known, you avoid repeating the noun:

    Instead of saying: **Mary** said **Mary** bought **the car**, now **the car** is **Mary's**.
    We say: **She** said **she** bought **it**, now **it** is **hers**.

In English:

Personal pronouns	Possessive pronouns	Reflexive pronouns	Object pronouns
I	mine	myself	me
you	yours	yourself	you
he, she, it	his, hers, its	himself, herself, itself	him, her, it
we	ours	ourselves	us
you	yours	yourselves	you
they	theirs	themselves	them

In Spanish:

Personal Pronouns (1)	Possessive pronouns (2)	Reflexive Pronouns (3)		Object Pronouns (4)
yo	mío	a mí mismo/a,	me	me, mí, conmigo
tú	tuyo	a ti mismo/a,	te	te, ti, contigo
él, ella	suyo/a	a él/ella mismo/a,	se	lo, la, le, se, él, ella
nosotros/as	nuestro/a	a nosotros mismos/as,	nos	nos, nosotros
vosotros/as	vuestro/a	a nosotros mismos/as,	os	os, vosotros
ellos/as	suyo/a	a ellos/as mismos /as,	se	los, las, les, se, ellos/as

Notes:

(1) For clarity, the personal pronouns "usted" and "ustedes" are not in the table. They mean you, singular and plural respectively; but they follow the verb as if they were "él" and "ellos", respectively.

> **He is** Perivian and **you are** Chilean.
> **Él es** peruano y **usted es** chileno.

(2) Don't confuse possessive pronouns (mine, yours, etc.) with possessive determiners:

English	Spanish
my	mi
your	tu, su (= de usted)
his, her, its	su
our	nuestro
your	vuestro (Spain), su (de ustedes)
their	su

(3) In Spanish reflexive pronouns can be simple (me, te, etc.) or redundant (a mí mismo, a ti mismo, etc.). If you use the redundant form, you have to use both.

> Have you seen **yourself** in the mirror?
> ¿**Te** has visto en el espejo? –simple–
> ¿**Te** has visto en el espejo **a ti mismo**? –redundant–

(4) For the third persons (so, él, she, it, they), Spanish distinguishes two types of direct pronouns: direct and indirect. For now, use this rule: Use only "lo/ la" or "los/ las," and if you encounter two lo, la, los, las; change the first one for "se."

> I have seen **her** in the cafeteria.
> **La** he visto en la cafeteria.

> I have written it **to them**.
> **Se** lo he escrito. (instead of ~~Los lo~~ he escrito)

When the pronoun is preceded by a preposition different from "con" (= with), the pronouns are: mí, ti, él, nosotros, vosotros ellos.

When the pronoun is preceded by the preposition "con" (=with), the pronouns are: conmigo, contigo, (con) él/rlls, (con) nosotros, (con) vosotro, (con) ellos.

11. GRAMMAR RULES

Golden Rule

> **Personal pronouns** are normally omitted. **Possessive pronouns** are normally placed the same way as English. **Reflexive and Object pronouns** can normally go in the beginning of the sentence.

Examples:

I am at home.
(yo) Estoy en casa.

This house is **mine.**
Esta casa es **mía.**

I am washing **myself.**
(yo) **Me** estoy lavando.

He is going to see **me** tomorrow.
(Él) **me** va a ver mañana.

This is for **me.**
Esto es para **mí.**

He is coming with **me.**
(Él) está viniendo **conmigo.**

Adverbs

Adverbs answer the questions: how, where and when. Unlike adjectives, which give information about nouns, adverbs give information about verbs.

They are reducing the cost of the product effective**ly**.
Están reduciendo el coste del producto eficaz**mente**.

Golden Rule

> Adverbs function in a similar way as adjectives. The main difference is that adverbs are invariable: They don't change masculine/feminine or singular/plural.

Example:

Pedro está trabajando **eficazmente**. **María** está trabajando **eficazmente**.
Pedro is working **effectively**. **Maria** is working **effectively**.

Prepositions

Prepositions are grammatical words: they don't have a "tangible" meaning, only a structural value in the sentence they are in. They can be single-word prepositions: at, in, on, over, under, below, etc., or multiple-word expressions functioning as prepositions, as "on top of, " or "in the middle of."

Golden Rule

> Prepositions always link parts of the sentence, and they can never go at the end of the sentence. Unlike English, they are never a part of a verb.

For example:

I am <u>calling off</u> the meeting for you.
Estoy cancelando la cita para ti

What are you <u>looking for</u>?
¿Qué estás <u>buscando</u>?

Conjunctions

Conjunctions are grammatical words that join two elemental clauses to create a compound sentence:

I studied enough. |and| I passed the test.
CLAUSE 1   CLAUSE 2

Golden Rule

> The translation English-Spanish is quite straightforward. For example, in every instance that you use "and," you can translate it by "y."

11. GRAMMAR RULES

Verbs

Verbs are the nuclei of the sentence. A sentence can lack nearly anything but a verb. Verbs are all those words that describe what the subject (the person or thing) does. The simplest form of a verb is called "infinitive." The infinitive is also the representative form of the verb. In English it is preceded by the word "to;" in Spanish it always ends in –ar, -er, -ir.

> to repeat, to posses, to declare, to prefer, to toast
> repet**ir**, pose**er**, declar**ar**, prefer**ir**, tost**ar**

Other that the infinitive (and two more), the tenses of the verbs change according to the subject: I, you, he, she, etc.

Golden Rule

The personal pronouns (yo, tú, él, etc.) are normally omitted because the verb contains that information in its ending. These endings are:		
English	Spanish	Example
I	–VOWEL or –y	plane**o**, so**y** (= **I** plan, **I** am)
you (singular)	–s	invita**s** (= **you** invite)
he/she/it	–VOWEL	cuent**a** (= **he/she/it** counts)
we	–mos	convence**mos** (= **we** convince)
you guys (Spain)	–is	aparecé**is** (= **you guys** appear)
you guys / they	–n	estudia**n** (=**you/ they** study)

General Vocabulary

Possessive pronouns

English	Spanish
mine	mío/ a
yours (singular)	tuyo/ a
his, hers, its	suyo/ a
ours	nuestro/ a
yours (plural) theirs -Spain-	vuestro/ a
yours (plural) theirs	suyo/ a

Object pronouns

English	Spanish
to/ at me	me
to/ at you (singular)	te
to/ at him, her, it	lo, la, le, se
to/ at us	nos
to/ at you (plural) -Spain-	os
to/ at you (plural), them	los, las, les, se

Pronouns with the preposition "con" (= with)

English	Spanish
with me	conmigo
with you (singular)	contigo
with him, her, it	con él, con ella
with us	con nosotros
with you (plural) -Spain-	con vosotros
with you (plural), them	con ustedes, con ellos/ as

Pronouns with other prepositions, e.g. para (= for)

English	Spanish
for me	por mí
for you (singular)	para ti
for him, her, it	para él, para ella
for us	para nosotros
for you (plural) -Spain-	para vosotros
for you (plural), them	para ustedes, para ellos/ as

Medical Vocabulary

Symtoms

English	Spanish
symptom	(el) síntoma
abrasion	rozadura, raspadura
anxiety	(la) ansiedad
asphyxia	asfixia
bite (from dog, etc.)	mordedura
bite (from mosquito, etc)	picadura
bruise	(el) moratón, (el) hematoma
blister	ampolla
bump	(el) chichón
burn	quemadura
congestion	(la) congestión
constipation	estreñimiento
contraction	(la) contracción
cough	(la) tos
cramp	(el) calambre
cut	(el) corte
diarrhea	diarrea
fever	(la) fiebre
inflammation	(la) inflamación
irritation	(la) irritación
itching	(la) picazón
lump	bulto
menstrual pain	(el) dolor menstrual
nausea, dizziness	náusea, mareo
pain, ache	(el) dolor
palpitations, tachycardia	(las) palpitaciones, taquicardia
pimple	grano
runny nose	moqueo
sleep	sueño
sneeze	estornudo
sting	picadura
sunburn	quemadura solar
swelling	(la) hinchazón
unusual tiredness	fatiga, cansancio
vomiting	vómito

12. NEGATIONS AND QUESTIONS
NEGACIONES Y PREGUNTAS

Negative Sentences

To convert a sentence into negative you just need to add the word "no" before the verb.

>That acrobatics does <u>not appear</u> possible.
>Esa acrobacia <u>no parece</u> posible.
>
>Juan is <u>not going</u> to cancel an interview.
>Juan <u>no va</u> a cancelar una entrevista.

In Spanish, you have to use a double negative. The exception is when the negative words: "nunca," "nadie," or "ninguno" (= never, nobody, none) are placed before the verb.

>Juan has **never** cancelled an interview.
>Juan **no** ha cancelado una entrevista **nunca**.[double negation]
>Juan **nunca** ha cancelado una entrevista. [single negation]
>**Nunca** Juan ha cancelado una entrevista. [single negation]
>
>Nobody administers that office.
>No administra esa oficina **nadie**.[double negation]
>**Nadie** administra esa oficina. [single negation]

Ninguno has three forms "ninguno," "ninguna" and "ningún." Use the latter when you name the object.

12. NEGATIONS AND QUESTIONS

No patient has cancelled the appointment.
Ningún paciente ha cancelado la cita.

None has cancelled the apponinment.
Ninguno ha cancelado la cita.

Notice that sentences using "nunca," "nadie" or "ninguno/a" (or ningún) are singular.

Nobody administers that office.
Nadie administra esa oficina.
Nadie ~~administran~~ esa oficina.

Interrogative Sentences

Unlike English, converting a sentence into interrogative requires only to put the right intonation.

If the question has a question word (what, where, when, which, etc), the **subject** normally goes after the verb.

At what time is **the director** leaving the hospital?
¿A qué hora está saliendo del hospital **el director**?

Otherwise (when there's no interrogative word), the location of the **subject** is optional

Is **Carlos** going to study at the library?
¿**Carlos** va a estudiar a la biblioteca?
¿Va **Carlos** a estudiar a la biblioteca?
¿Va a estudiar **Carlos** a la biblioteca?
¿Va a estudiar a la biblioteca **Carlos**?

Interrogative-Negative Sentences

When a sentence is both negative and interrogative, the rules of above overlap.

Has Juan never canceled an interview?
¿Juan **no** ha cancelado una entrevista **nunca**?
¿Juan **nunca** ha cancelado una entrevista?
¿**Nunca** Juan ha cancelado una entrevista?

General Vocabulary

Adverbs for negations and questions

English	Spanish
yes	sí
if	si
no, not	no
never	nunca
nobody	nadie
none, no...	ninguno/ a, ningún
What...?	¿Qué ...?
Which...?	¿Cuál/ Cuáles...?
Who...?	¿Quién/ Quiénes...?
Where...?	¿Dónde...?
When...?	¿Cuándo...?
How...?	¿Cómo ...?
How much...?	¿Cuánto/ a...?
How many...?	¿Cuántos/ as...?
(for) How long...?	¿(durante) Cuánto tiempo...?
How long ago...?	¿Cuánto tiempo hace que...?
How often...?	¿Con qué frecuencia...?
Since when...?	¿Desde cuándo...?

12. NEGATIONS AND QUESTIONS

Medical Vocabulary

Tools and procedures of diagnostics

English	Spanish
tool	herramienta
procedure	procedimiento
diagnostics	(el) diagnóstico
analysis	(el) análisis
biopsy	biopsia
blood test	(el) análisis de sangre
catheter, probe	(el) catéter, sonda
cotton ball	(el) algodón
CT scan	(el) TAC *
echocardiogram	ecocardiografía, (el) ecocardiograma
endoscopy	endoscopia
eye drop	colirio
gloves	(el) guante
MRI	(el) IRM **, tomografía
mammogram	mamografía, mamograma
mask	mascarilla
microscope	microscopio
monitor	(el) monitor
needle	aguja
ruler	regla
sample	muestra
scalpel	escalpelo, (el) bisturí
scissors	(las) tijeras
stethoscope	estetoscopio
syringe	jeringuilla
suture	sutura
test	prueba, (el) test
thermometer	termómetro
ultrasonography	ultrasonido, ecografía
urine analysis	(el) análisis de orina
weight scale	peso, balanza
X ray	(los) rayos X (ekis)

(*) TAC stands for Tomografía Axial Computarizada
(**) IRM stands for Imagen por Resonancia Magnética

SECTION IV

VERBS
VERBOS

So far you know three structures of verbs: I am singing, I have sung, and I am going to sing (Estoy cantando, He cantado, Voy a cantar). In this section we will add some verbs to shape some very useful structures (as those used to give instructions and recommendations).

You will learn that Spanish verbs can express: an action that falls on oneself (as in English in "I wash myself"), or an action without a subject (as in English in "Something appeals to me").

Later this section will introduce the present tense (I sing), and the past tense (I sang), and will give you some details on how to deal with the irregular verbs.

The last chapter, *Chapter 17 Next Steps in Spanish*, will provide you with a perspective on where you are in your learning: what you have learned, and what is ahead.

13. VERY IMPORTANT VERBS
VERBOS MUY IMPORTANTES

"Ser" and "Estar" (= to be)

Remember the conjugation of the verbs "ser" and "estar."

	ser	estar
(I)	soy	estoy
(you singular)	eres	estás
(he/she/it)	es	está
(we)	somos	estamos
(you guys)- Spain-	sois	estáis
(you guys/ they)	son	están

In *Chapter 9 One Future, Present, and Past*, you saw the forms of "estar" (estoy, estás, etc.) to build structures as: Estoy cantando (= I am singing); but this verb can also stand used alone, without another verb.

You will use "estar" as "to be" when the attribute is temporary, for example:

>**I am** content.
>**Estoy** contento.

But "to be" has another translation, "ser". The verb "ser" is used when the attribute is permanent.

>**I am** from Peru.
>**Soy** de Perú.

13. VERY IMPORTANT VERBS

Warning

> Certain expressions that use "to be" in English, use another verb in Spanish: "tener."

For example:

> **I am** hungry/ thirsty/ hot/ cold/ sleepy/ twenty years old.
> **Tengo** hambre/ sed/ calor/ frío/ sueño/ veinte años.

Don't confuse the present tense you have studied (I am singing) with the "simple present" (I sing). The form "I am singing "combines the simple present of the verb "to be," with the gerund of the verb in question (here, to sing).

"Haber" and "Tener" (= to have)

Remember:

	haber	tener
(I)	he	tengo
(you singular)	has	tienes
(he/she/it)	ha	tiene
(we)	hemos	tenemos
(you guys) -Spain-	habéis	tenéis
(you guys/ they)	han	tienen

As explained *in Chapter 9 One Future, Present and Past*, the verb "haber" (he, has, ha, etc.) is an auxiliary verb, and it does not have a meaning. It is just used to build structures as: He cantado (= I have sung).

> **He** establecido un récord.
> **I have** established a record.

On the contrary, "tener," although it's equivalent "to have," has a concrete meaning, as "to have got."

> **Tengo** [tener] un problema
> **I have** a problem.

The expression "I have to" in Spanish uses the verb "tener," not "haber."

> I've got to cancel the tickets.
> Tengo que cancelar los tiquets.

"Ir" (= to go)

Remember:

	ir
(I)	v<u>o</u>y
(you singular)	vas
(he/she/it)	va
(we)	v<u>a</u>mos
(you guys)- Spain-	v<u>a</u>is
(you guys/ they)	van

As *Chapter 9 One Future, Presen, and Past* explained, the form of "ir" (voy, vas, etc.), to build structures as: Voy a cantar (= I am going to sing). But this verb can also be used alone, as a simple verb, for example:

>Voy a la oficina en carro.
>I go to the office by car.

"Hay" and "Queda" (= *there is* and *there is left*)

To express "there is/ there are," Spanish uses "hay."

>**There is** water in my car.
>**Hay** agua en mi carro.

"Hay" is an impersonal form of the verb "haber." Impersonal means that there's no person doing the action. To use other tenses as "there was" or "there will be," you simply have to use the pattern of the verb "haber ."

>**There was** water in my car.
>**Había** agua en mi carro.
>
>**There were** two doctors available at that time.
>**Había** dos doctores disponibles en ese momento.
>
>**There will be** a solution.
>**Habrá** una solución.

Likewise is "queda"

>**There is** water **left** in the bottle.
>**Queda** agua en la botella.

13. VERY IMPORTANT VERBS

There are lemons **left** in the basket.
Quedan limones en la cesta.

"Poder" (= can, may) and "tener que" (= to have to)

The following is a table with all forms in the present tense for "poder."

	poder
(I)	puedo
(you singular)	puedes
(he/she/it)	puede
(we)	podemos
(you guys)- Spain-	podéis
(you guys/ they)	pueden

As *Chapter 9 One Future, Present and Past* explained, how to build sentences in those three tenses, but this is not enough to express **commands and recommendations.**

As in English, Spanish has a tense to express commands, as "Come this way." But the simplest way to convey a message that implies an order or a recommendation is to use the equivalent of "can" and "to have to."

Thus, for example, "Come this way" will become: "Can you come this way;" or "Take this pill" will become: "You have to take this pill."

Can you come this way.
Puedes venir por aquí.

You have to take one pill every six hours.
Tienes que tomar una píldora cada seis horas.

Notice that some forms of "poder" have **ue** despite the infinitive (poder) has an **o**: puedo, puedes, etc.

"Deber" (= to ought to) and "necesitar" (= to need)

The following is a table with all forms in the simple present for "deber" and "necesitar."

	deber	necesitar
(I)	d<u>e</u>bo	neces<u>i</u>to
(you singular)	d<u>e</u>bes	neces<u>i</u>tas
(he/she/it)	d<u>e</u>be	neces<u>i</u>ta
(we)	deb<u>e</u>mos	necesit<u>a</u>mos
(you guys)- Spain-	deb**éis**	necesit**áis**
(you guys/ they)	d<u>e</u>ben	neces<u>i</u>tan

These two verbs help build sentences to express **commands and recommendations.**

> **You need** one pill every six hours.
> **Necesitas** una píldora cada seis horas.
>
> **You need** to take one pill every six hours.
> **Necesitas** tomar una píldora cada seis horas.
>
> **You ought to take** one pill every six hours.
> **Debes** tomar una píldora cada seis horas.

These two verbs (deber and necesitar) are **regular**. This means that they follow the table of Spanish endings with no exceptions. The following is the table of endings for the simple present, for verb in AR, ER, IR:

	AR	ER	IR
(I)	o	o	o
(you singular)	as	es	es
(he/she/it)	a	e	e
(we)	amos	emos	imos
(you guys)- Spain-	áis	éis	ís
(you guys/ they)	an	en	en

13. VERY IMPORTANT VERBS

Irregular Verbs

A verb is **regular** when follows exactly all the endings that correspond to its conjugation. If a given verb has one single irregularity in just one tense, it is enough to call it **irregular**.

To illustrate what an irregular verb is, let's compare the regular verb "deber" with the irregular verbs "tener" and "ser."

The following table shows one column with the endings of the regular verbs in ER in the present tense, and the other columns with the forms of the verb "deber" (regular), and "tener" and "ser" (both irregular)

	Endings of ER verbs	deber	tener	ser
(I)	o	debo	ten**g**o	so**y**
(you singular)	es	debes	t**ie**nes	**er**es
(he/she/it)	e	debe	t**ie**ne	**es**
(we)	emos	debemos	tenemos	s**o**mos
(you guys)- Spain-	éis	debéis	tenéis	s**o**is
(you guys/ they)	en	deben	t**ie**nen	s**o**n

Note: The shading corresponds to those forms that are irregular. The frame indicates the irregularity.

General Vocabulary

Elements of a hospital room

English	Spanish
element	elemento
hospital	(el) hospital
room	(la) habitación
air conditioning	aire acondicionado
bath	baño
bath tub	bañera
bed	cama
blanket	manta, cobija
carpet	alfombra, moqueta
chair	silla
closet	armario
computer	computadora
curtain	cortina
drawer	(el) cajón
glass, cup	vaso
hanger	perchero
heater	(la) calefacción
lamp	lámpara
mattress	(el) colchón
mug	taza
pillow	almohada
remote	mando a distancia
seat	asiento
sheet	sábana
shower	ducha
sofa	(el) sofá
stretcher	camilla
table	mesa
telephone	teléfono
television	(la) televisión
toilet	inodoro
tray	bandeja
ventilator, fan	(el) ventilador

13. VERY IMPORTANT VERBS

Elements of a hospital

English	Spanish
hospital	(el) hospital
ambulatory	ambulatorio
building	edificio
cafeteria	cafetería
ceiling	techo
corridor	pasillo
chapel, meditation room	capilla, sala de meditación
delivery room	sala de partos
department of pediatrics	departamento de pediatría
door	puerta
E.R.	sala de emergencias
emergency clinic	clínica de urgencias
entrance	entrada
exit	salida
express clinic	clínica exprés
floor, storey	piso, planta
floor, ground	suelo
garage	(el) garaje
intensive care	(los) cuidados intensivos
laboratory	laboratorio
maternity ward	sala de maternidad
parking area	(el) área de aparcamiento
pharmacy	farmacia
quiosk	quiosco
reception	(la) recepción
rehab. room	sala de rehabilitación
restrooms	(los) baños, (los) servicios
room	(la) habitación, sala, cuarto
shop	tienda
surgery room	quirófano
waiting room	sala de espera
wall	(la) pared
window	ventana
window (of assistance)	ventanilla
wing of the building	(el) ala del edificio

Medical Vocabulary

Disorders and diseases

English	Spanish
disorder	(el) desorden
disease	(la) enfermedad
addiction	(la) adicción
AIDS	(el) SIDA
alcoholism	alcoholismo
allergy	alergia
Alzheimer	(el) Alzheimer
amnesia	amnesia
anorexia	anorexia
arthritis	(la) artritis
asthma	(el) asma
astigmatism	astigmatismo
atrophy	atrofia
avian flu	(la) gripe aviar
bacteria	bacteria
bronchitis	(la) bronquitis
cancer	(el) cáncer
cataracts	(las) cataratas
chickenpox	varicela
cirrhosis	(la) cirrosis
clot	coágulo
cold	resfriado, constipado
dementia	demencia
depression	(la) depresión
diabetes	(la) diabetes
diphtheria	difteria
Down syndrome	(el) síndrome de Down
drug addiction	(la) drogadicción
flea	pulga
flu	(la) gripe
fracture	fractura
fungi	(los) hongos
gonorrhea	gonorrea
heart attack	(el) ataque al corazón
heart murmur	soplo
hepatitis	(la) hepatitis
herpes	(los) herpes

13. VERY IMPORTANT VERBS

English	Spanish
HIV	(el) VIH *
insomnia	insomnio
louse	piojo
meningitis	(la) meningitis
migraine	migraña
mumps	(las) paperas
myopia	miopía
obesity	(la) obesidad
osteoporosis	(la) osteoporosis
otitis	(la) otitis
paralysis	(la) parálisis
Parkinson	(el) Parkinson
peritonitis	(la) peritonitis
pharyngitis	(la) faringitis
phlebitis	(la) flebitis
pneumonia	neumonía
reflux	reflujo
rheumatism	reumatismo
scoliosis	(la) escoliosis
shingles	(los) herpes zóster
STD	(la) enfermedad de trasmisión sexual
stress, anxiety	(el) estrés, (la) ansiedad
stroke	(el) ataque cerebral
syphilis	(la) sífilis
tetanus	(el) tétanos
thrombosis	(la) trombosis
tuberculosis	(la) tuberculosis
typhus	(el) tifus
tumor	(el) tumor
varicose veins	(las) varices
venereal disease	(la) enfermedad venérea
virus	(el) virus
wart	verruga
whooping cough	(la) tos ferina

(*) VIH stands for virus de inmunodeficiencia humana

14. TRANSLATING "IT APPEALS TO ME"
TRADUCIENDO "ME GUSTA"

The verbs of the family of "gustar" (= to appeal, to like) are those that are conjugated the other way round, and the indirect object functions as the subject of the clause, and vice versa. There are verbs like those in both Spanish and English.

>That idea appeals to **me** (not: ~~I appeal that idea~~).
>Esa idea **me** gusta. (not: ~~Yo gusto esa idea~~).

For the purpose of making an analogy, we translated "gustar" as to appeal; although its meaning is closer to "to like:"

>I like that idea
>Esa idea **me** gusta.

Another example of verbs of this type is "doler" (= to hurt)

>This needle is going to hurt you. (not: ~~You are going to hurt it~~)
>Esta aguja va a dolerte. (not: ~~Tú vas a dolerte esta aguja~~).

In order to use these verbs, you need to know the pronouns that substitute the person in the sentence. These are:

English	Spanish	English	Spanish
me	me	It appeals to me.	Me gusta.
you (singular)	te	It appeals to you.	Te gusta.
him/ her	le	It appeals to him.	Le gusta.
us	nos	It appeals to us.	Nos gusta.
you guys	os (Spain)	It appeals to you.	Os gusta.
you guys, them	les	It appeals to them.	Les gusta.

14. TRANSLATING "IT APPEALS TO ME"

Notes:
1. Notice that this list contains basically the same pronouns we saw in *Chapter 11 Grammar Rules*.
2. Remember that, when using "usted" and "ustedes", you have to use the forms "le" and "les."
3. Remember that always the content in the fifth cell of our six-cell tables refers to the equivalent "you guys" which is used only in Spain.

Both English and Spanish have a few verbs with this peculiarity of being conjugated in the reverse. The problem is that they are not the same. For example, the verb "gustar" (= to like):

> You are going to like tennis.
> Te va a gustar el tenis.

The Optional Emphasis in the Person

In *Chapter 7 Conjugation*, we learned to put the personal pronoun (yo, tú, él...) in a sentence to emphasize who does the action.

> "I" am going to have that responsibility.
> "Yo" voy a tener esa responsabilidad.

With verbs of the family of "gustar" when you want to put emphasis on the person that makes the action, you cannot use the personal pronoun (since the subject of the sentence is not the person but the "thing"). So, instead, you will use the expressions below in addition of the pronouns: me, te, le, etc.

Spanish	English
a mí	me
a ti	you
a él, a ella	him, her
a nosotros/ as	us
a vosotros/ as (Spain)	you
a usted, a ellos/ as	them

Example:

> Recently soccer is fascinating 'you,' not 'me.'
> Recientemente, **a ti** te está fascinando el fútbol, no **a mí**.

The order of the sentence

You can alter the order of subject and object, as long as the verb follows the conjugation of the actual object.

>Esa idea me está atrayendo. = Me está atrayendo esa idea.
>That idea is attracting me. = It's attracting me, that idea.

>Not "Esa idea estoy atrayendo" or "Estoy atrayendo esa idea."

Tips

Exercise

The majority of verbs of the family of "gustar" are regular. By using the endings of the simple present and the General Vocabulary of this chapter, translate the sentences below.

	AR	ER	IR
(I)	o	o	o
(you singular)	as	es	es
(he/she/it)	a	e	e
(we)	amos	emos	imos
(you guys)- Spain-	áis	éis	ís
(you guys/ they)	an	en	en

I like driving.
I don't care if you like it or not.
We are interested in investing in the market of plastics.
Does the nomination surprise you?
They love soccer.

Answers

>Me gusta manejar.
>No me importa si te gusta o no.
>Estamos interesados en (= Nos interesa) invertir en el mercado de los plásticos.
>¿Te sorprende el nombramiento?
>Les encanta el fútbol.

14. TRANSLATING "IT APPEALS TO ME"

General Vocabulary

Useful verbs of the *gustar* family

English	Spanish
to appeal to	atraer *
to be afraid of	dar miedo *
to be left, as in "There's one pill left"	quedar
to be sore, as in "My neck is sore"	doler *
to care, as in "I don't care"	importar
to dislike, as in "I dislike that plan"	disgustar
to feel like	apetecer *
to feel shame	dar * vergüenza, pena
to feel sorry	dar pena *
to find, as in "I find this cheap"	parecer *
to get annoyed	enojar
to get astonished	asombrar
to get bothered	molestar
to get fascinated	fascinar
to get indignant	indignar
to get offended	ofender
to get surprised	sorprender
to give motivation	motivar
to have an opinion about something	resultar
to have fun	divertir *
to like someone/ to dislike someone	caer * bien/ mal
to like, as in "I like playing guitar"	gustar
to love, as in "I love playing guitar"	encantar
to panic	dar pánico *
to revolt	dar asco *, repugnar

(*) irregular verb

Notice that the infinitive of all verbs in Spanish end in "ar," "er," "ir," and the stress is always in the last vowel.

Administrative data

English *	Spanish
administrative data	datos administrativos
name	(el) nombre, nombre y apellido
first name	(el) nombre, nombre de pila
last name	apellido
maiden name	(el) nombre de soltera
middle name	(el) segundo nombre
ID	(la) identificación
driving license	permiso de conducir
passport	(el) pasaporte
medical card	tarjeta médica
business card	tarjeta de negocio
credit card	tarjeta de crédito
vaccination card	tarjeta de vacunación
photo	(la) foto
SS number	número de la seguridad social
birth date	fecha de nacimiento
age	(la) edad
insurance	seguro
employer	(el) empleador
manager	(el) jefe
address	(la) dirección
street	(la) calle
city	(la) ciudad
ZIP	código postal
state	estado
country, nation	(el) país
telephone	teléfono
cell	(el) celular, (el) móvil
email	(el) email (same pronunciation)
form	formulario
representative	(el) representante
contact person	persona de contacto
marital status	estado civil
sex, gender	sexo

(*) Not in alphabetical order

Medical Vocabulary

Drugs

English	Spanish
drug	medicamento
anesthesia	anestesia
anti depressive	antidepresivo
antacid	antiácido
antibiotic	antibiótico
anticoagulant	(el) anticoagulante
antidote	antídoto
antihistaminic	antihistamínico
aspirin	aspirina
contraceptive pill	píldora anticonceptiva
cough syrup	(el) jarabe para la tos
epidural	(la) epidural
oxytocin, pitosin	oxitocina
vaccine	vacuna

Tools of treatment and prevention

English	Spanish
treatment and prevention	tratamiento y prevención
bandage	venda
band-aid	curita, tirita
capsule	cápsula
condom	(el) condón, preservativo
cream	crema
gel	(el) gel
intubation	sonda
IV, saline	suero, suero fisiológico
lotion	(la) loción
ointment	pomada
oxygen mask	mascarilla de oxígeno
paste	pasta
pill	píldora, pastilla,
powder	(los) polvos
serum	suero
syringe	jeringuilla
syrup	(el) jarabe
tablet	tableta, pastilla

15. REFLEXIVITY AND PASSIVE VOICE
REFLEXIVIDAD Y VOZ PASIVA

In this chapter we will analyze other roles that the pronouns (me, you, him, etc.) can play with verbs. These cases are:

1) Reflexivity. When the action falls on the same subject that does the action.

> Little Pedro washes himself.
> Pedrito **se** lava.

2) Passive Voice. When the object over which the action falls becomes the subject. Unlike English, Spanish inserts a pronoun.

> The car is washed.
> El carro **se** lava.

For clarity –and for you to practice- the examples in this chapter use extensively the present tense "I sing" instead of "I am singing."

Remember the table of endings of the present tense:

	AR	ER	IR
(I)	o	o	o
(you singular)	as	es	es
(he/she/it)	a	e	e
(we)	amos	emos	imos
(you guys)- Spain-	áis	éis	ís
(you guys/ they)	an	en	en

15. REFLEXIVITY AND PASSIVE VOICE

Reflexivity

With many verbs, one can act on oneself (I wash myself). When a verb functions this way it is called reflexive. Notice that these verbs can act on something in the same way that they can act on themselves.

Let's take the verb to bathe (= bañar) as an example. A person can either act on something (the Direct Object) or on oneself.

>I bathe my 3-month old baby. / I bathe myself (I have a bath)
>(yo) Baño a mi bebé de 3 meses. / Me baño.

When a verb acts on itself, we say that the verb, in that use, is reflexive. In its reflexive form, the infinitive adds the particle **-se**, e.g. bañar**se** (= to bathe oneself, to have a bath).

>Having a bath is a pleasure.
>Bañarse es un placer.

>They have a bath in the river.
>(ellos) Se bañan en el río.

>They bathe each other in the river.
>(ellos) Se bañan en el río.

For clarity, we will call "reflexive" all verbs that follow the pattern shown above. Strictly speaking, some of them are called "pronominal verbs," as "arrepentirse" (= to repent).

Reflexive verbs can be classified into four types.

Type One. Verbs that function as either reflexive or not depending on the direct object being oneself or something else.
Note: In Spanish you can use the reflexive pronoun and the object in the same sentence: Me lavo el pelo (I wash "myself" my hair). e.g. lavar (= to wash).

>I wash my car in the garage.
>Lavo mi coche en el garaje.

>I wash myself with very warm water.
>Me lavo con agua muy caliente.

Most of the verbs of this category behave the same in Spanish and English

Type Two. Verbs that function as either reflexive or non-reflexive optionally, depending on the speaker's style. Reflexive style is more colloquial or implies more affection, e.g. comer (= to eat).

>I eat my lunch in half an hour.
>Como mi almuerzo en media hora.
>
>I eat my lunch in half an hour.
>Me como mi almuerzo en media hora.

Examples are: morir, olvidar, caer, escapar (= to die, to forget, to fall, to escape).

Type Three. Verbs that can function as either reflexive or not depending on the meaning, e.g. empeñar (= to insist/ to pawn).

>He insists in going.
>(Él) se empeña en ir.
>
>I have to pawn my jewels.
>Tengo que empeñar mis joyas.

Another example is: negar/ negarse (to deny/ to refuse).

Type Four. Verbs that can only function as reflexive, e.g. quejar (= to complain).

>This doesn't work: I am going to complain.
>Esto no funciona: me voy a quejar.

Examples are: arrepentirse, fugarse, atreverse, suicidarse (= to repent, to flee, to dare, to commit suicide).

15. REFLEXIVITY AND PASSIVE VOICE

The Passive Voice

A sentence is in passive voice when you have swapped the subject with the object, e.g.:

<u>The nurse</u> controls <u>the machine</u> at distance. (ACTIVE VOICE)
SUBJECT   OBJECT

<u>The machine</u> is controlled by <u>the nurse</u> at distance. (PASSIVE V.)
SUBJECT   OBJECT

Spanish also has that structure:

<u>La enfermera</u> controla <u>la máquina</u> a distancia.

<u>La máquina</u> es controlada por <u>la enfermera</u> a distancia

But Spanish prefers to use the pronoun "**se**" for this structure, and to omit the real subject (nurse).

The machine is controlled at distance.
La máquina se controla a distancia.

Or: Se controla la máquina a distancia.

It's believed that that method works.
Se cree que ese método funciona.

Tips:

Use of: To get/ become + Adjective/ Past Participle

Sentences that express a transition as: I get sick, I get nervous (versus I'm sick, I'm nervous) are commonly translated in Spanish by the verb "ponerse" (literally: to put oneself).

(yo) pongo, (tú) pones, (él) pone, (nosotros) ponemos, (vosotros) ponéis, (ellos) ponen
I put, you put, s/he puts, we put, you guys, they put.

I become sick. I get nervous.
Me pongo enfermo. Me pongo nervioso.

General Vocabulary

Some verbs that can function as reflexive

English	Spanish
to bathe someone	bañar
to bathe oneself	bañarse
to bore someone	aburrir
to get bored	aburrirse
to comb someone	peinar
to comb oneself	peinarse
to dress someone	vestir *
to get dressed	vestirse *
to dry someone or sth.	secar
to get dried	secarse
to get up someone	levantar (a alguien)
to get up	levantarse
to meet with someone	quedar con (alguien)
to stay	quedarse
to put	poner *
to put on (clothes)	ponerse *
to take away	quitar
to take off (clothes)	quitarse
to shave someone	afeitar
to shave oneself	afeitarse
to tire someone	cansar
to get tired	cansarse
to try, to taste	probar *
to try clothes on	probarse *
to upset someone	enojar
to get upset	enojarse
to wake up someone	despertar * (a alguien)
to wake up oneself	despertarse *
to wash someone	lavar
to wash oneself	lavarse

(*) irregular verb

15. REFLEXIVITY AND PASSIVE VOICE

Medical Vocabulary

Procedures of treatment

English	Spanish
treatment procedure	procedimiento de tratamiento
acupressure	(la) acupresión, digitopuntura
acupuncture	acupuntura
amputation	(la) amputación
blood transfusion	(la) transfusión de sangre
chemotherapy	quimioterapia
circumcision	(la) circuncisión
CPR	(la) RCP *
dialysis	(la) diálisis
dressing	vendado
hydration	(la) hidratación
massage	(el) masaje
medication	(la) medicación
physiotherapy	fisioterapia
psychotherapy	psicoterapia
radiotherapy	radioterapia
rehabilitation	(la) rehabilitación
reimplantation	(el) reimplante, (la) reimplantación
resuscitation	(la) reanimación
RICE **	descanso, hielo, (la) compresión, elevación
skin graft	injerto de piel
surgery	cirugía
suture	sutura
therapy	terapia
tourniquet	(el) torniquete
transplant	(el) trasplante
vasectomy	vasectomía

(*) RCP stands for Reanimación Cardio-Pulmonar
(**) RICE stands for Rest, Ice, Compressión, Elevation

16. THE PRESENT AND PAST TENSES
LOS TIEMPOS PRESENTE Y PASADO

So far you have learned three tenses. Let's review this with the verb "to sing." We have one present (I am singing), one past (I have sung), and one future (I am going to sing).

These three tenses are compounded and are formed with more than one verb.

I am singing	(to be + to sing)
I have sung	(to have + to sing)
I am going to sing	(to be + to go + to sing)

These tenses are the simplest. Once you know the auxiliary verbs involved (the equivalents in Spanish to "to be," "to have," and "to go"), you don't need much more.

Paradoxically, the simple tenses (those that involve only one verb) are more difficult, because you have to deal with the irregularities of the verb that you are using (and there are many verbs).

In this chapter we will see:

- the **regular** verbs in the **present tense** (I sing)
- the **regular** verbs in the **past tense** (I sang)
- the **false-irregular** or spelling-changing verbs
- the **irregular** verbs

16. THE PRESENT AND THE PAST TENSES

Regular Verbs in the Present Tense

The following is the table of endings of the present tense of the regular verbs.

	AR Verbs	ER Verbs	IR Verbs
(I)	-o	-o	-o
(you singular)	-as	-es	-es
(he/she/it)	-a	-e	-e
(we)	-amos	-emos	-imos
(you guys)- Spain-	-ais	-eis	-ís
(you guys/ they)	-an	-en	-en

When you apply those endings to the three model verbs, the result is:

	cantar	beber	partir
(I)	canto	bebo	parto
(you singular)	cantas	bebes	partes
(he/she/it)	canta	bebe	parte
(we)	cantamos	bebemos	partimos
(you guys)- Spain-	cantáis	bebéis	partís
(you guys/ they)	cantan	beben	parten

We marked the person in parentheses to indicate that, in Spanish, it is redundant. You don't need to say: "Yo canto" (= I sing), just "Canto."

Examples of use of the present tense:

> I sing, you sing, he sings, we sing, you guys sing, you/ they sing
> canto, cantas, canta, cantamos, cantáis (Spain), cantan
>
> I drink, you drink, he drinks, we drink, you drink, you/they drink
> bebo, bebes, bebe, bebemos, bebéis (Spain), beben
>
> I live, you live, he lives, we live, you guys live, you/they live
> vivo, vives, vive, vivimos, vivís (Spain), viven

Unlike English, Spanish can use the present tense to describe historical facts.

> Columbus discovered America in 1492.
> Colón descubre America en 1492.

Regular Verbs in the Past Tense

The following is the table of endings of the present tense of the regular verbs.

	AR Verbs	ER Verbs	IR Verbs
(I)	-é	-í	-í
(you singular)	-aste	-iste	-iste
(he/she/it)	-ó	-ió	-ió
(we)	-amos	-imos	-imos
(you guys) - Spain-	-asteis	-isteis	-isteis
(you guys/ they)	-aron	-ieron	-ieron

When you apply those endings to the three model verbs, the result is:

	cantar	beber	partir
(I)	canté	bebí	partí
(you singular)	cantaste	bebiste	partiste
(he/she/it)	cantó	bebió	partió
(we)	cantamos	bebimos	partimos
(you guys) - Spain-	cantasteis	bebisteis	partisteis
(you guys/ they)	cantaron	bebieron	partieron

False-irregular or Spelling-changing Verbs

It may happen that the verb needs to alter its spelling to accommodate the right pronunciation. An example is **vencer** (= to defeat). If we add the endings to form the present tense, we obtain a wrong pronunciation of its forms. Venc-er /benthér/ → it should sound /benth-o/, but ~~venco~~ gives /benko/ instead.

	vencer
(I)	venzo
(you singular)	vences
(he/she/it)	vence
(we)	vencemos
(you guys)-Spain-	vencéis
(you guys/ they)	vencen

16. THE PRESENT AND THE PAST TENSES

If you take the stem venc- and then add the suffix -o, the result is venco, but the "c" with "o" doesn't sound as "s" of vencer. That's why the spelling needs to change.

This happens with the verbs ending in:

-cer → -zo
-cir → -zo
-ger → -jo
-gir → -jo
-guir → -go
-quir → -co

Warning

> You don't have to memorize these endings. As you learn the rules of spelling of this book, you will notice when you write them (remember: pronunciation wise, they are regular). Notice that it is the same tranformation of:
> poco (= little of) + ito → poquito (= little bit of), not ~~pocito~~

Examples:

	-cer → -zo	-cir → -zo	-ger → -jo
	vencer	esparcir	proteger
	= to defeat	= to spread	= to protect
(I)	venzo	esparzo	protejo
(you singular)	vences	esparces	proteges
(he/she/it)	vence	esparce	protege
(we)	vencemos	esparcimos	protegemos
(you guys)-Sp.	vencéis	esparcís	protegéis
(you guys/ they)	vencen	esparcen	protegen

	-gir → jo	-guir → -go	quie → -co
	exigir	distinguir	delinquir
	= to demand	= to distinguish	= to commit a crime
(I)	exijo	distingo	delinco
(you singular)	exiges	distingues	delinques
(he/she/it)	exige	distingue	delinque
(we)	exigimos	distinguimos	delinquimos
(you guys)-Sp.	exigís	distinguís	delinquís
(you guys/ they)	exigent	distinguen	delinquen

Also notice that these alterations can also happen when the verb is irregular for other reasons. For example "seguir" (= to follow) is irregular (not what we called "false irregular"). The present tense "sigo" (I follow) changes its stem; and in addition, it needs to alter its "u" to accommodate to the right pronunciation, according to the above rules ("sigo," not ~~siguo~~).

These alterations only take place with the Present tense and Present Subjunctive (Present Subjunctive is not covered in this book).

The Irregular Verbs

Remember what we saw in *Chapter 7 Conjugation,* the infinitive (as "to sing") is the prime form of the verb and also its representative.

Every variation of a verb is called "the form" of the verb. Thus, for example, the infinitive "to sing" has several forms: sing, sang, sung. In Spanish, verbs have many forms.

Remember that all Spanish infinitives end in AR, ER, IR, with no exception. What is left in the verb when you remove AR, ER, IR is called the stem. Thus, **the stems** of the verbs: cant**ar**, beb**er**, and viv**ir** (to sing, to drink, to live) are: cant, beb, viv.

Each form of a verb can be broken down into two parts: the stem and the ending.

        canto = cant + o   (I sing)
        cantamos = cant + aremos (We sing)

A form can be irregular for three different reasons: 1) because the stem changes, 2) because the ending changes, or 3) because both change.

In the intermediate course *Spanish for Californians: Using English to Learn Spanish* you will learn about irregular verbs in detail. For now, **what is important is that you learn how to recognize the infinitive** out of any form you hear (in order to identify its meaning or to be able to find its meaning in the dictionary). For example, imagine you know the word "pintar" (= to paint), and your patient says: "Pintamos casas" (= We paint houses), you should recognize, a least, the infinitive "pintar."

16. THE PRESENT AND THE PAST TENSES

For this purpose, the following classification of irregular forms will be helpful:

- **Irregular form because of changes in its ending**

    A form can be irregular due to a transformation of its ending. For example the present tense of "distribuir" is "distribuyo," not ~~distribuo~~." The stem "distribu" hasn't changed.

    Since here the stem doesn't change, you should have no **problem to recognize its infinitive** ("distribuir").

- **Irregular form because of changes in its stem**

    A form can be irregular due to a transformation of its stem. There are two very common transformations (from what it should be if regular to what really is) **o → ue** and **e → ie**. For example the present tense of contar (= to count) is "cuento" (I count), not "~~conto~~." Another example: the present tense of the verb preferir (= to prefer) is "prefiero (= I prefer), not "~~prefero~~."

    Knowing this should help you **recognize the infinitive** of the form. Now, if you hear forms as "cuento" or "prefiero," you can expect than the infinitives will be "contar," and "preferir." And remember: the form that you will find in the dictionary is the infinitive (contar = to count; preferir = to prefer).

- **Irregular form because of changes in both, ending and stem**

    A form can be irregular due to a transformation of both ending and stem. There are only three verbs with forms having an **unrecognizable infinitive**: haber, ser, and ir. Thus, for example, from the forms "he" (= I have just…), eres (= you are), or voy (= I go), you cannot deduce that their infinitives are: "haber," "ser," or "ir," respectively. This is why you should get very familiar with these verbs.

	haber	ser	ir
(I)	he	soy	voy
(you singular)	has	eres	vas
(he/she/it)	ha	es	va
(we)	hemos	somos	vamos
(you guys)- Spain-	habéis	sois	vais
(you guys/ they)	han	son	van

General Vocabulary

General Questions

We recommend that you learn some useful sentences that can't be translated literally. Learn each structure as is.

>What's your name? My name is Antonio Smith.
>¿Cómo te llamas? Me llamo Antonio Smith.
>
>How old are you? I'm 40 years old.
>¿Cuántos años tienes? Tengo 40 (cuarenta) años.
>
>Where are you from? I'm from San Jose, California.
>¿De dónde eres? Soy de San José, California.
>
>How long have you been here? I've been here for 3 years / I've been here since 2009.
>¿Cuánto tiempo llevas aquí? Llevo aquí tres años. / Llevo aquí desde el 2009.
>
>How long ago did you work there?
>¿Cuánto hace que trabajaste allí?
>
>How often do you take your medicine?
>¿Con qué frecuencia tomas tu medicina?
>
>What's the time?
>¿Qué hora es?
>
>What's your date of birth?
>¿Cuál es tu fecha de nacimiento?
>
>What's your telephone?
>¿Cuál es tu teléfono?

Notice that all these sentences above use the conjugation of "tú" (you-informal) as in "¿Cómo te llamas?", instead of "usted", as in "¿Cómo se llama?" . The phasebook at the end of this volume, uses "usted" (you-formal), to expose you to that form

16. THE PRESENT AND THE PAST TENSES

Medical Vocabulary

Accidents and incidents

English	Spanish
accident	(el) accidente
incident	(el) incidente
car accident	(el) accidente de carro
cardiac arrest	paro cardiaco
choking	atragantamiento
explosion	(la) explosión
fall	caída
fight	pelea
fire	incendio
overdose	(la) sobredosis
respiratory arrest	paro respiratorio
shooting	tiroteo
stabbing	puñalada
strangulation	(la) estrangulación
stroke	(el) derrame cerebral

Units

English	Spanish
unit	(la) unidad
amp	amperio
cubic centimeter	centímetro cúbico
degree (of temperature)	grado (de temperatura)
feet	(el) pie
gallon	galón
gram/ milligram/ kilogram	gramo/ miligramo/ kilogramo
inch	pulgada
liter/ milliliter	mililitro
meter/ millimeter/ centimeter	metro/ milímetro, centímetro
millimeter of mercury	milímetro de mercurio
ounce	onza
pound	libra
square centimeter	centímetro cuadrado
volt	voltio

17. NEXT STEPS IN SPANISH
PASOS SIGUIENTES EN EL ESPAÑOL

What have you learned

These are the skills you have:

- **You can read**. You may not understand everything you read, but you can read every quick note in Spanish. On the spot, when talking with a patient, you can communicate a certain word you don't know by using your pocket dictionary and be able to read it properly.

- **You can write**. You may misspell words (~~pasiente~~ instead of paciente; or ~~ora~~ instead of hora), but everything you write will be understandable. On the spot, you can memorialize data (directions, a prescription, etc.).

- **You can use the dictionary efficiently**. You can find words quickly in your future learning. You can also convert texts or quick notes no matter which changes are in the words, no matter the word being feminine (e.g. amarilla instead of amarillo -yellow) , plural (e.g. carros instead of carro –cars vs. car) or a conjugated form (e.g. "canto" instead of "cantar" – I sing vs. to sing).

- **You can greet and express immediate messages.** You know many stand alone sentences as: hola, adiós, uno, sí, cuidado, or okey (= hello, goodbye, one, yes, watch out, OK)

17. NEXT STEPS IN SPANISH

- **You can make statements and questions about the past, present, and future**. You may not understand the tense of your speaker yet, but you can convey any message and "conjugate" in a past, present, or future tense.

- **You can give instructions and recommendations.** You can use the equivalents of "to need," "to have to" and "can."

This gives you enough tools to start communicate in the context of a health care provider that addresses a patient, but most importantly, this knowledge is the foundation of Spanish.

What to remember

The Spanish in this book is not all of it. It is limited to the medical setting. It is good that you know your strengths:

- **You control the conversation**. You are the one that asks the questions, so you can set the language level of the conversation. For instance, if you use the tense "Have you done…?" the speaker will tend to answer the same way ("Yes, I have done…or I haven't done…" (instead of "I did").

  This is why this book focuses on those tenses that are the simplest to learn and use.

- **You know the context.** You know the protocol of a medical visit, from the greeting to the departure.

  This is why this volume includes a phrasebook sorted by the settings: 1) getting the patient's history, 2) examining and diagnosing, 3) procedures and treatments, and 4) teaching and follow up.

- **You are a health care professional already.** You are the one that knows the message that needs to be conveyed to the patient.

  For this reason the method of this book doesn't impose the words you are going to learn. You are the one that knows what needs to be asked and said to the patient.

- **You can speak English already**. English has many commonalities with Spanish. Many Spanish words (medical and non medical) are similar to their English counterpart. In addition, the patient may know some English; so, with caution, words in English can be used as a last resource.

  This is why this book: is in English, uses similar words in English in its examples, and has lists of words in alphabetical order in English.

- **You can always ask the patient.** You can ask the patient to repeat or to put in writing the words you didn't catch.

  This is one of the reasons why the first chapters of this book teach you how to read and write first.

- **You know the basic Spanish you need.** You don't need to know words of slang or any deviation of the language. If the patient doesn't speak a standard Spanish, you must request a professional interpreter (who may also struggle).

  This is why this book only uses normative Spanish: the standard used in all Spanish-speaking countries.

- **You know the basic medical Spanish you need.** You don't need a very technical vocabulary. The patients don't know technical terms. The words you need to acquire are just those that you expect to use and hear with your patients.

  This is why this book focus just in that Spanish heard in medical settings; and it provides just the vocabulary in the health field that a patient commonly knows and understand.

17. NEXT STEPS IN SPANISH

What is out there

We have identified **six elements that** can be obstacles in learning for the English-speaker.

1. Objects have gender (*Chapter 6 Masculine/ Feminine*).
2. There are two verbs for "to be;" "ser" and "estar" (*Chapter7 Conjugation*).
3. Verbs are conjugated; and some verbs are irregular (*Chapter7 Conjugation*).
4. Pronouns can appear in pairs - I will tell that to him (*Chapter 11 Grammar Rules*).
5. There are two types of past tense: the preterite and the imperfect past. E.g. "I **sang** yesterday" vs. "I **used to sing**").
6. There are two extra tenses; they are called the present subjunctive and the past subjunctive. E.g. "It is important that you **are** here tomorrow" vs. "It is important that you **be** here tomorrow").

After completion of this book, the natural next step would be a grammar course at the intermediate level. We recommend the book *Spanish for Californians*, where you will learn:

- **More Grammar Structures.**

    What this book calls "rules of thumb" have exceptions. For example the rule of thumb that the pronouns can be placed in front of the verb is true, but in some cases, they can be placed after the verb.

    > I am going to need **him** tomorrow.
    > **Lo** voy a necesitar mañana [option 1].
    > Voy a necesitar**lo** mañana [option 2].

    In this regard, the book *Spanish for Californias: Using English to Learn Spanish* devotes one chapter for each part of the speech (nouns, adjectives, verbs, etc.).

- **More Verbal Tenses**

    You will learn different ways to communicate ideas in the present, past or future. This book limits itself to one form for each tense (The equivalents of: "I am doing." "I have done," "I am going to do"). These are the simplest in Spanish; there are others. For example

    > I **am going to** need him tomorrow.
    > Lo voy a necesitar mañana.
    >
    > I **will** need him tomorrow.
    > Lo necesitaré manana.

    This includes the tenses that become more problematic in Spanish: **the subjuctive tenses.**

    > I am going to suggest that he **use** it. (vs. "uses")
    > Voy a sugerir que lo **use** (vs. "usa")

    The book *Spanish for Californians* analyzes the use of each verb tense, classifies its irregularities, as well as it provides a table with the irregular verbs and its types of irregularities.

Tips

Frequently Asked Questions

FAQ 1: Where can I find sentences to practice?

> Nowadays, there are many free resources available online; but the simplest is the Phrasebook in this book. These phrases come from real life and they are consistant with what you have learned in this book.

FAQ 2: Where can I learn about dialects and cultural differences?

> There are two appendices at the end of this book focusing on the three major dialectal variations within Spanish language (Spain, Latin America, and Argentina), and some cultural features that Spanish-speaking countries have in common.

General Vocabulary

Adjectives used with "ser:" conditions

English	Spanish
allergic (e.g. I am allergic.)	alérgico/a (e.g. Soy alérgico.)
asthmatic	asmático/a
blind	ciego/a
chronic	crónico/a
color blind	daltónico/a
contagious	contagioso/a, infeccioso/a
deaf	sordo/a
mute	mudo/a
grave	grave
hereditary	hereditario/a
one-eyed	tuerto/ a
paraplegic	parapléjico/a
toxic	tóxico/a

Adjectives used with "estar:" states

English	Spanish
asleep (e.g. He's asleep.)	dormido/a (e.g. Está dormido.)
clean	limpio/a
crazy	loco/a
dead	muerto/a
dirty	sucio/a
handicapped	discapacitado/a
healthy	sano/a
ill	enfermo/a
in comma	en coma
in shock	en shock
infected	infectado/a
intoxicated	intoxicado/a
sane	cuerdo/a
sterile	estéril

Verbs

English	Spanish
to admit	dar * el alta
to anesthetize	anestesiar
to ask	preguntar
to ask for	pedir *
to be in pain	doler *
to breastfeed	dar * el pecho
to break up waters	romper la fuente, romper aguas
to clean	limpiar
to cure, to heal	curar
to cut	cortar
to discharge	dar * el alta
to dress	vestirse *
to feel	sentir *
to get better	mejorar
to get worse	empeorar
to give	dar *
to hear	oír *
to hurt	herir *, hacer * daño
to inform	informar
to lay down	echarse, acostarse *
to let go	soltar *
to operate	operar
to measure	medir *
to move	mover *
to press	presionar
to put	poner *
to remove	quitar
to sedate	sedar
to see	ver *
to sit down	sentarse
to take out	sacar
to touch	tocar
to undress	desvestirse *
to weigh	pesar

(*) irregular verb

Medical Vocabulary

Miscellaneous nouns

English	Spanish
ambulance	(el) ambulancia
appointment	cita
artificial leg, arm	(la) pierna, brazo artificial
baby	(el) bebé
cast	escayola
cell	célula
chocking	atragantamiento
crutches	(las) muletas
delivery	parto
DNA	(el) ADN (a-de-ene)
embryo	(el) embrión
fetus	feto
fireman	bombero
immunity	(la) inmunidad
infant	(el) lactante
infection	(la) infección
investigation	(la) investigación
newborn	(el) recién nacido
pace maker	(el) marcapasos
patient	(el) paciente
poison	veneno
policeman	(el) policía
prescription	receta médica
prevention	(la) prevención
prognosis	(la) evolución esperada
referral	(el) volante
result	resultado
statistics	estadística
tattoo	(el) tatuaje
toxin	toxina
venom	veneno
visitor	visita
wheel chair	silla de ruedas

Adjectives

English	Spanish
arterial (e.g. arterial problem)	arterial (e.g. problema arterial)
bacterial	bacteriano
blood (blood related)	sanguíneo
bronchial	bronquial
bucal	bucal
cardiac	cardíaco
cerebral	cerebral
dental	dental
hepatic	hepático
intestinal	intestinal
lymphatic	linfático
medical	médico
muscular	muscular
nasal	nasal
ocular	ocular
pancreatic	pancreático
prostatic	prostático
psychiatric	psiquiátrico
pulmonary	pulmonar
rectal	rectal
renal	renal
vaginal	vaginal
venous	venoso
viral	viral

Note: As explained in *Chapter 11 Grammar Rules*, unlike English, the Spanish adjectives are placed after the noun:

problema arterial = arterial problem

In addition to this, in most cases, you have the option to mean the same using "de" (= of) and the corresponding noun (In English the corresponding noun of "arterial" is "artery"):

problema de arteria = artery problem

PHRASEBOOK

PHRASEBOOK

A phrasebook contains useful expressions and their translations. This phrasebook is classified in four standard stages of a visit:

- Getting a History
- Assesment/ Diagnosis
- Procedures
- Teaching/ Follow up

Some phrases include either common patient answers or comments on the grammar. The patern used is the following:

> **#. Question in English**
> Question in Spanish
>
> **Answer in English**
> Answer in Spanish
>
> Notes on grammar

All phrases use the form "**usted**" instead of "tú."

The translations are **not literal**. The Spanish phrases resort to what you learned in this book. Thus, for example :

> **#29 Did you pass out?** →
> ¿Se ha desmayado? , whose literally translation would be: "Have you pased out?"
>
> **#42 Open your mounth.** →
> ¿Puede abrir la boca?, whose literally translation would be: "Can you open your mounth?"

Getting a history

1. **Hello, my name is Ana. I am a nurse. I am going to be working with you today.**
   Hola, me llamo Ana . Soy enfermera. Voy a estar trabajando con usted hoy.

   > Note: "Me llamo" is literally "I call myself."

2. **I am going to ask you some questions before the medical exam.**
   Voy a hacerle unas preguntas antes del reconocimiento médico.

3. **What is your relationship with that person?**
   ¿Cuál es su relación con esa persona?

4. **Your visitor must wait outside. I'm going to ask you personal questions.**
   Su acompañante debe esperar fuera. Voy a preguntarle preguntas personales.

5. **What is your name?**
   ¿Cómo se llama?

   > **My name is Antonia Agüero Vargas.**
   > Me llamo Antonia Agüero Vargas.
   >
   > Notes: 1 "Me llamo" is literally "I call myself". 2. In many Spanish-speaking families there are two last names.

6. **How do you spell that?**
   ¿Cómo lo deletrea?

   > **Ana Hernández, as it sounds. With "z" and "h"**
   > Ana Hernández, como suena. Con zeta y hache.
   >
   > Note: "s" sound can be spelt with "s," "z" or "c."

7. **What is your address?**
   ¿Cuál es su dirección?

   > **24, 10th St., San Rafael, California.**
   > Calle diez, número veinticuatro, San Rafael, California.

Notes: 1. You can expect that the patient will say first the street number. 2. Rafael would be: /rah-fah-ehl/.

8. **Can you write that down?**
    ¿Lo puede escribir?

    I don't know how to spell it in English.
    No sé cómo se deletrea en inglés.

    Notes: 1. Sé (with accent mark) is the present tense of "saber," irregular. 2. "Se deletrea" means is "it is spelt" (see *Chapter 15 Reflexivity and Passive Voice*).

9. **What is your phone number?**
    ¿Cuál es su teléfono?

    My cell is, area code 510 676-1101.
    Mi celular es código de área quinientos diez, seis siete seis, once cero uno.

    Note: You can expect different groupings of figures, as: cinco, uno, cero…

10. **Can you say one number at a time**
    Puede decir los números uno a uno

11. **What is your date of birth?**
    ¿Cuál es su fecha de nacimiento?

    March 2, 1960.
    "2/3/1960" Dos de marzo de mil novecientos sesenta

    Note: 1. Make sure it is left clear what figure represents day and month –See *Appendix B Notes About Culture*.

12. **Have you been here before?**
    ¿Ha estado aquí antes?

    I have never been here.
    No he estado aquí nunca.

    Note: Double Negative (see *Chapter 12 Negations and Questions*).

13. **This is a consent to be treated here.**
    Esto es un consentimiento para ser atendido aquí.

14. **I need your signature / initials.**
    Necesito su firma/ sus iniciales.

15. **This is information about your privacy rights and patient rights.**
    Ésta es información sobre sus derechos de privacidad y derechos del paciente.

16. **Who can we contact in case of emergency? name and phone number.**
    ¿A quién podemos contactar en caso de emergencia? nombre y número de teléfono

    > **No, I don't know anyone.**
    > No, no conozco a nadie.
    >
    > Note: "conozco" is present tense, the verb "conocer" is irregular.

17. **Would you like me to call your family?**
    ¿Quiere que llame a alguien de su familia?

    > **No, thanks, My sister comes with me. She is parking the car.**
    > No, gracias. Mi hermana viene conmigo. Está estacionando el carro.
    >
    > Notes: Literally means: "Would you like me to call someone of your family." 2. "Quiere", "viene" are simple present, "querer" and "venir" are irregular.

18. **I am going to measure your temperature and weigh you.**
    Voy a tomarle la temperatura y pesarle.

19. **I am going to take your pulse/ preassure.**
    Voy a tomarle el pulso/ la presión sanguínea.

20. **Why are you here today?**
    ¿Por qué esta aquí hoy?

    > **My stomack hurts very much.**
    > Me duele mucho el estómago.

Note: Me duele is literally "It hurts." The verb "doler" is irregular, and of the family of "gustar" *(Chapter 14 Translating "It Appeals to me")*.

21. **What happened?**
    ¿Qué pasó?

    > **I tripped and cut my lip.**
    > Tropecé y me corté el labio.
    >
    > Note: "Me corté" is literally "I cut myself."

22. **How long has this been going on?**
    ¿Cuánto tiempo lleva así?

    > **Since Tuesday. For two days.**
    > Desde el martes. Dos días.
    >
    > Notes: 1. Literally, "How long have you been like this." 2. "Llevar tres días" is "to take three days."

23. **What medical problems do you have? Diabetes?**
    ¿Qué problemas médicos ha tenido: Diabetes?

    > **I have high blood pressure and I had a stroke.**
    > Tengo presion alta y he tenido un infarto.

24. **Does your family have a history of heart desease?**
    ¿Su famlia tiene un historial de problemas del corazón?

    > **Yes, my father died of a heart attack**
    > Sí, mi padre murió de un ataque al corazón.

25. **Do you take any medications regularly? Did you take any medications today?**
    ¿Está tomando algún medicamento regularmente? ¿Ha tomado algún medicamento hoy?

    > **Yes, some pills for my stomach.**
    > Sí, unas pastillas para el estómago.
    >
    > Note: Some patients maynot consider "medicina" a drug sold over the counter.

26. **Have you taken any over-the-counter medication?**
    ¿ha tomado algún medicamento que no necesita receta?

    > **Yes, tylenol**
    > Sí, tylenol

    > Note: "medicamento que no necesita receta" means liteally medicine that doesn't need presciption.

27. **When was your last menstrual period?**
    ¿Cuándo ha sido su última menstruación?

    > **I still have menstruation. It started yesterday.**
    > Todavía tengo la regla. Empezó ayer.

28. **Are you pregnant / dizzy / bleeding/ nauseaus?**
    ¿Está embarazada/ mareada/ sangrando/ con náuseas?

    > **Yes, I have vomited this morning.**
    > Si, he vomitado esta mañana.

    > Note: "Está con náuseas" or "Tiene náuseas."

29. **Did you pass out?**
    ¿Se ha desmayado?

    > **No, but I feel very tired.**
    > No, pero me siento muy cansada.

    > Note: "Me siento" is literally "I feel myself". "Se ha desmayado" is literally "Have you passed out yourself."

30. **Did someone hurt you?**
    ¿Alguien le ha hecho daño?

    > **Nobody has hit me.**
    > Nadie me ha pegado.

Assessment / Diagnosis

31. **Are you in pain now?**
    ¿Le duele algo ahora?

    > Not any more.
    > Ya no.

32. **Where is you pain?**
    ¿Dónde le duele?

    > Here, in the stomach.
    > Aquí, en el estómago.

    > Note: body language

33. **What type of pain? dull, sharp, pulsating, cramping...?**
    ¿Qué tipo de dolor? Leve, agudo, intermitente, como un calambre?

    > It's a pain that comes and goes, and as if it burns.
    > Es un dolor que viene y se va, y como si me quemara.

34. **How much it hurts, in a scale 0 to 10? 0 is no pain, 10 is the highest.**
    ¿Cuánto le duele, en una escala de cero a diez? Cero es sin dolor, 10 es lo más fuerte.

    > Eight.
    > Ocho.

35. **Have you been vomiting, diarrhea, nausea? How many times?**
    ¿Ha estado vomitando, con diarrea o con náusea? ¿Cuántas veces?

    > No, in fact I have constipation.
    > No, de hecho tengo estreñimiento.

    > Note: "tengo estreñimiento" o "estoy estreñido."

36. **When did it start?**
    ¿Cuándo ha comenzado?

    > One week ago.
    > Hace una semana.

    > Note: "ha comenzado" literally: "it has started."

37. **Are you having trouble breathing?**
    ¿Está teniendo problemas para respirar?

    > **No, I am not.**
    > No.

38. **Do you need to sleep with pillows? How many?**
    ¿Necesita dormir con almohadas? ¿Cuántas?

    > **I sleep with four pillows.**
    > Duermo con cuatro almohadas.

39. **Is that normal for you?**
    ¿Es eso normal para ti?

    > **No, just this week.**
    > No, sólo esta semana.

40. **Do you get short of breath walking? How far? Stairs?**
    ¿Se queda sin aliento al caminar? ¿Cuánto puede caminar? ¿Sube escaleras?

    > **I get short of breath easily. I can only walk 5 minutes.**
    > Me fatigo fácilmente. Puedo caminar nomás cinco minutos.

41. **Do you have pain when exercising?**
    ¿Le duele cuando hace ejercicio?

42. **Open your mouth**
    ¿Puede abrir la boca?

43. **Take a deep breath**
    ¿Puede tomar aire profundamente?

44. **Hold your breath. Now, breath normally.**
    ¿Puede mantener el aire? Ahora ya puede respirar normalmente

45. **Sit here.**
    Puede sentarse aquí

46. **Remove your clothes, put on this gown**
    ¿Puede quitarse la ropa y ponerse esta bata?

47. **Take off your shirt (pants, bra)?**
    ¿Puede ponerse la camisa (pantalones, sujetador)?

48. **You can take your clothes back on.**
    Se puede poner la ropa.

49. **Laydown.**
    ¿Puede echarse?

50. **I will press on your stomach.**
    Voy a presionar su estómago.

51. **Your blood sugar is high. This is a sign of diabetes.**
    Su nivel de azúcar en sangre es alto. Esto es una señal de diabetes.

52. **You have an infection in you bladder (stomach, skin, lungs...).**
    Usted tiene una infección en la vejiga (estomago, piel, pulmones).

53. **Your lab work is abnormal...**
    Su analítica no es normal.

54. **We need to do further testing (lab, xray, CT, MRI, ultrasound...).**
    Necesitamos hacer más tests (un test de laboratorio, unos rayos equis, un TAC, una resonancia, un ultrasonido).

55. **You need surgery.**
    Necesita cirugía.

56. **Your appendix (spleen, etc.) is injured (infected, swollen, etc.)**
    Su apéndice (bazo,...) está dañado (infectado, inflamado,...)

57. **We are going to check your vital signs after you walk.**
    Vamos a comprobar sus signos vitales después de caminar.

Procedures

58. **I am going to listen to your heart (lungs).**
    Voy a escuchar su corazón (pulmón).

59. **We will need to draw blood.**
    Vamos a necesitar sacar sangre.

60. **I am going to place a catheter, a tube to drain your urine.**
    Voy a poner un catéter, un tubo para drenar orina.

61. **I will start an IV and give you fluid.**
    Voy a comenzar un intravenoso y suministrarle suero.

62. **I need you to give a urine (stool) sample.**
    Necesito que usted haga una muestra de orina/ de heces.

Teaching / follow up

63. **You have an appointment on march first, here.**
    Usted tiene una cita el uno de marzo, aquí.

64. **You need to change your dressing twice a day.**
    Usted necesita cambiar su vendaje dos veces al día.

65. **You need to take esta pildora and to take exercise, to walk.**
    Usted necesita tomar esta pastilla y hacer ejercicio, caminar.

66. **This medication may make you drowsy (nauseous, constipated).**
    Esta medicación puede que le produzca sueño (náusea, estreñimiento).

67. **Cut down on salt, fat, sugar, in your diet.**
    Debe quitar la sal, la grasa, el azúcar de su dieta.

68. **You should not eat after midnight.**
    No debe comer después de la medianoche.

69. **Do not eat salt at all.**
    No puede tomar nada de sal.

70. **You must drink a lot of water.**
    Debe tomar mucha agua.

71. **I have sent a referral to the specialist. You will have surgery next week.**
    He enviado un volante a su especialista. Usted va a tener cirugía la semana próxima.

72. **Do you have any questions?**
    ¿Tiene alguna pregunta?

73. **Do you have someone to drive you home?**
    ¿Tiene alguna persona para llevarle en carro a casa?

74. **You need to return if you have more pain, vomiting or bleeding.**
    Necesita regresar si tiene más dolor, vómitos o sangre.

    > Note: "vómitos o sangre" literally means "vomit and blood."

75. **The drain will be removed at your follow up visit next week.**
    El drenaje le va a ser quitado en su visita de seguimiento la próxima semana.

76. **No work for three weeks.**
    No debe trabajar durante tres semanas.

77. **You need to exercise five times a week. You could walk for twenty minutes.**
    Necesita hacer ejercicio cinco veces a la semana. Debes caminar durante veinte minutos.

78. **Losing weight will help you control your diabetes.**
    Perder peso va a ayudarle a controlar su diabetes.

    > Note: "Perder" is used instead of "perdiendo" when the word is not functioning as a verb. Notice that in this example the verb is "help," not "losing."

79. **You should weigh yourself every morning and write it down.**
    Debe pesarse cada mañana y anotarlo.

80. **No heavy lifting for two weeks.**
    No debe levantar nada pesado en dos semanas.

APPENDICES

APPENDIX A

NOTES ABOUT DIALECTS
NOTAS SOBRE DIALECTOS

APPENDIX A: NOTES ABOUT DIALECTS
NOTAS SOBRE DIALECTOS

All languages have dialects. In the same way that English speakers from United Kingdom, Ireland, United States or Australia speak the same language differently; speakers from Spain, Argentina or Mexico have recognizable differences.

Nonetheless, Spanish is a very unified language. The rules of grammar and spelling are the same all over the Spanish-speaking world. The differences between dialects are limited mostly to the preference of some words over others, and some differences in the pronunciation.

English	Example 1	Example 2
US English	line	tomato /tomeito/
UK English	queue	tomato /tomatoh/
Spanish		
Mexican Spanish	fila (= line)	jitomate (= tomato)
Spanish from Spain	cola	tomate

The Spanish spoken in the southwest of United States (mostly California, Arizona, Texas and New Mexico) belongs for the most part, to the realm of the Mexican dialect. In addition, the Spanish in the US is, of course, influenced by the English language, and some words used are not part of the standard.

APPENDIX A. NOTES ABOUT DIALECTS

	Example 1	Example 2	Example 3
English	market	carpet	truck
Non-standard Spanish	marketa	carpeta	troca
Spanish	mercado	alfombra	camión

A language can be divided into dialects and, in turn, those dialects can be subdivided into subdialects indefinitely. However, we can consider three main dialects with the following representatives:

- the Spanish from Spain
- the Spanish from Latin America except Argentina
- the Spanish from Argentina

The most apparent difference among the dialects in Spanish is the use of the pronouns and the verb forms thereof, as shown in the following table:

	Spain	**Latin America**	**Argentina**
I sing	(yo) canto	← THE SAME	← THE SAME
You (singular) sing	**(tú) cantas**	← THE SAME	**(vos) cantás** *
He/ She sings	(él /ella) canta	← THE SAME	← THE SAME
We sing	(nosotros) cantamos	← THE SAME	← THE SAME
You guys sing	**(vosotros) cantáis**	**(ustedes) cantan**	← THE SAME
They sing	(ellos) cantan	← THE SAME	← THE SAME

* Notice that the stress is on the last "a."

When addressing someone **formally**, the pronouns used are the same in all three dialects:

	Spain	**Latin America**	**Argentina**
sir/ ma'am, you sing	(usted) canta	← THE SAME	← THE SAME
sirs/ ma'ams, you sing	(ustedes) cantan	← THE SAME	← THE SAME

Thus, only in Spain there is a distinction for the plural form "you:" *vosotros* (informal), *ustedes* (formal).

Spanish from Spain

Except in the Southern area, Spain uses the English *th* **sound** for both the letter **z**, and the letter **c** when combined in **ce**, **ci** (as is explained in this book).

In Spain, they use **vosotros** (= you guys). "Vosotros" is one form taught in this book. In Spain, they also use "usted" (= you singular) and "ustedes" (= you plural), but only either to mark a distance from the person you are addressing, like addressing a stranger, or to show respect, like addressing a professor.

Usted uses the forms of "él/ella," e.g. "Usted estudia mucho." In the same way, "ustedes" uses the forms of "ellos," e.g. "Ustedes estudian mucho."

Only in Spain it is used the forms of the second person of plural, and its pronouns, which are:

"**vosotros**" (or vosotras) as in "**vosotros** cantáis" (= you guys study). In Latin America: "**ustedes** cantan."

"**vuestro**" (or "vuestra," "vuestros," "vuestras") as in "vuestro amigo" (= the friend of you guys). In Latin America: "**Su** amigo."

"**os**" as in "Os veo" (= I see you guys). In Latin America: "**Los** veo."

A rule to use the forms of **vosotros** is simply to substitute the ending "mos" of **nosotros** for "is." Thus,

Nosotros canta**mos** → Vosotros cantáis
Nosotros bebe**mos** → Vosotros bebéis
Nosotros viví**mos** → Vosotros vivís

(= We sing, drink, live -- You guys sing, drink, live)

This rule works for most of the irregular verbs too, e.g. dormir (= to sleep)

Nosotros dormi**mos** → Vosotros dormís

APPENDIX A. NOTES ABOUT DIALECTS

There are three exceptions:

a) The verb "haber" (= to have)

Nosotros he**mos** estudiado → Vosotros habé**is** estudiado
(no: Vosotros ~~heis~~ estudiado)

(= We have studied -- You guys have studied)

b) The nosotros form when ending in "imos". In this case, the vosotros form will have only one "I," e.g. :

Nosotros vivi**mos** → Vosotros vivís
(not: Vosotros ~~viviis~~)

(= We live -- You guys live)

c) The past tense. For this tense, the vosotros form can be created out of the "tú" form just by adding "is," e.g.:

Tú cantaste → Vosotros cantaste**is**
Tú bebiste → Vosotros bebiste**is**
Tú vivíste → Vosotros viviste**is**

Spanish from Latin America

In Latin America, they use the **/s/ sound** for the letter **c** when combined in **ce, ci,** and the letter **z** (instead of the /th/ sound used in Spain). So, they don't distinguish between "caza" (= hunting) and "casa" (= house), or between "coser" (= to sew) and "cocer"(= to boil).

Latin America **never uses "vosotros."** Instead, "ustedes" is used. Remember: **ustedes** uses the same forms of "ellos" e.g. Ustedes <u>estudian</u> mucho y ellos <u>estudian</u> poco (= You guys study a lot, but they study little).

In some areas of Latin American, they never use "tú." They use "usted" instead. Remember: "usted" uses the same forms of "él/ella" e.g. Usted <u>estudia</u> mucho y él <u>estudia</u> poco (= You study a lot, but he studies little).

Spanish from Argentina

In regards to the characteristics of Spanish spoken in Latin America, Argentina shows two specific differences: the use of **"vos,"** and the pronunciation of the **strong "ll."**

Argentina has a very strong pronunciation of both the "ll," and the "y" as a consonant. It sounds close to the English "g" in George or the "sh" in shoe, depending on the speaker.

Argentina uses vos (= you singular) instead of "tú." Generally speaking, "vos" goes with the forms of "vosotros" but eliminates the -i- of the last syllable. Example:

vosotros cantá~~i~~s → vos cantás.

This rule only applies for the simple present (vos cantás).

The commands –a tense not studied in this book- also makes a transformation from the original "vosotros." It uses the form of vosotros but eliminates the final "d."

Canta~~d~~ vosotros → cantá vos

Vos, for the rest of the tenses follow the standard rules of conjugation of "tú."

"Vos" does not have its own set of associated pronouns, so it uses the ones of "tú." Examples:

Vos, a **tu** manera… (= you, in your way, …).
A vos **te** canta María (= Maria sings to you).
No tenés que ir**te** (= You don't have to go).

The use of vos is called "voseo." Argentina is where voseo is norm. Uruguay, Paraguay and other areas of Latin America use "vos," but their rules are not consistent, as those in Argentina, and it is not considered standard.

APPENDIX B

NOTES ABOUT CULTURE
NOTAS SOBRE CULTURA

APPENDIX B: NOTES ABOUT CULTURE
NOTAS SOBRE CULTURA

In the process of communicating with a patient some knowledge about the culture of the speaker can be crucial. Below are some features that may be distinctive of the culture in the Spanish speaking countries.

1. Figures

Remember that the Spanish word **billón** doesn't mean *billion*. Instead, one **billón** equals 1000 billions.

        1,000,000,000 is one billion.
        1,000,000,000 es mil millones.

        1,000,000,000,000 is one thousand billion.
        1,000,000,000,000 es un billón.

Spanish never expresses figures neither in tens nor in hundreds.

        1900 is nineteen hundred.
        1900 es mil novecientos.

        1995 is nineteen, ninety five.
        1995 es mil novecientos noventa y cinco

Unlike English, in Spanish the comma is frequently used to indicate decimal and the period is used to indicate thousands.

Pi is 3.14 approximately.
Pi es 3,14 aproximadamente.

2,000 is two thousand.
2.000 es dos mil.

In Spanish, monetary figures have the symbol of the currency at the end.

2.000,50 $ son dos mil dólares con cincuenta centavos.
$2,000.50 is two thousand dollars and fifty cents.

2. Units of measurement

Many countries only use units of measurement of the International Systems (also called metric system, or decimal system).

Below is a table with the names of the units, their abbreviations, and their conversion to U.S. system units.

Abrev.	Spanish	English	Conversion
g	gramo	gram	1 g = 0.03 oz (onzas de peso)
Kg	kilo	kilo	1 Kg = 2.2 Lb (libras)
m	metro	meter	1 m = 3.28 ft (pies)
cm	centímetro	centimeter	1 cm = 0.39 inch (pulgadas)
Km	kilómetro	kilometer	1 Km = 0.62 miles (millas)
l	litro	liter	1 l = 0.26 gal (galones) 1 l = 33.81 fl oz (onzas de líquido)
°C	Celsius	Celsius	37 C = 98.6 °F (Fahrenheit) * 38 C = 100.4 °F 39 C = 102.2 °F

(*) The conversion from Celsius to Fahrenheit is not linear. The formulae is: °F = (°C x 9/5) + 32. The range 37 C to 39 C, of the table, corresponds to common fever.

3. Dates

Dates are given in this order: day, month, and year:
  01/31/12 is January thirty first, two thousand twelve.
  31/01/12 es el treinta y uno de enero de dos mil doce.

Years, as any figure, are **never** expressed in tens or hundreds. (See "Figures" above).

In Spanish calendars, the week starts on Monday –not on Sunday.

4. Tú vs. Usted

In those regions where both **tú** and **usted** are used (some regions only use usted), "tú" is used to address someone informally, and "usted" formally.

Every Spanish-speaking country has its different social codes, and they accept "tú" in different levels of familiarity. This is why it is recommended that you use "usted" always, unless the patient addresses you differently.

Usted is abbreviated as Ud. or Vd.; and **ustedes,** as Uds. or Vds.

5. Courtesy

Use **por favor** (= please) extensively. It could sound rude otherwise, specially with commands.

  Por favor, puedes venir por aquí (not: Ven por aquí).
  Please, can you come this way.

Smiling and using the courtesy tags will really help you gain your patient's confidence and respect.

  Gracias. De nada. Por favor. Lo siento
  Thank you. You're welcome. Please. I am sorry.

6. The two last names

In many Spanish speaking countries the naming system includes the father's and mother's paternal family names.

The first name, **el nombre** or **el nombre de pila** (= the Baptism name) can be one or more names, i.e. José Carlos, Marco Antonio.

The first surname, **el apellido**, or **el primer apellido**, or **el apellido del padre** (= the father's surname) is always the person's father's last name.

The second surname, **el segundo apellido**, or **el apellido de la madre** (= the mother's surname) is the person mother's last name.

For example, Antonio Álvarez Ala and Beatriz Barroso Barrio's have a child. They name him Luis. Consequently, Luis' full name is: Luis Álvarez Barroso.

7. The Pace of the Day

The stages of the day are: **la mañana**, which lasts from the sunrise until lunch time (at 1, 2 or even 3 pm); **la tarde**, until sunset; and **la noche**, when it's dark. So, Spanish doesn't distinguish between afternoon and evening. They both are **la tarde**.

The strongest meal of the day is commonly **la comida** or **el almuerzo** (= lunch). **El desayuno** and **la cena** (= breakfast and dinner) are lighter meals. All these meals are typically taken later than their counterparts in the English culture. In addition, people may have a snack before lunch, called **el aperitivo,** or before dinner, called **la merienda**.

Traditionally, people have a nap, **la siesta**, after lunch. It is believed that this tradition is a result of having a heavy meal and high temperatures at the time of that meal. One common characteristic of the Spanish-speaking countries is the hot climate. Spain enjoys hot summers; so does her sister countries in the Americas. Even Argentina and Chile, with extreme latitude, have regions with hot summers.

Nowadays, work schedules with long commutes and short lunch breaks don't allow time for this nap; however, in summertime and during holidays many people in those countries have a nap after lunch.

8. Greetings

It is extended in the Spanish-speaking world to give one **beso** (= kiss) or two on the cheeks as a way of greeting. The kiss exchange occurs woman-woman or man-woman, and it is used among family and friends.

The traditional formal manner to greet is a handshake; however, in a medical environment, it is perfectly acceptable not to offer a handshake.

9. Other Cultural Patterns

Many other cultural patterns in the Spanish speaking world can be found; however they are either local or not distinctive from other cultures or limited to certain social groups. This is the case of certain beliefs in healing procedures and drugs. Some people visit **hueseros** (= bone healers) or **santeros** (= faith healers) before or instead of visiting the doctor, or they go to **botánicas** or **herbolarios** (= herbal stores) before or instead of going to the pharmacy.

APPENDIX C

PRESENTE TENSE
EL PRESENTE DE INDICATIVO

APPENDIX C: PRESENT TENSE
EL PRESENTE DE INDICATIVO

Regular Verbs

	AR Verbs	ER Verbs	IR Verbs
(I)	-o	-o	-o
(you singular)	-as	-es	-es
(he/she/it)	-a	-e	-e
(we)	-amos	-emos	-imos
(you guys)- Spain-	-ais	-eis	-ís
(you guys/ they)	-an	-en	-en

	cantar	beber	partir
(I)	canto	bebo	parto
(you singular)	cantas	bebes	partes
(he/she/it)	canta	bebe	parte
(we)	cantamos	bebemos	partimos
(you guys)- Spain-	cantáis	bebéis	partís
(you guys/ they)	cantan	beben	parten

We marked the persons in parentheses to denote that in Spanish, it is redundant to put it because the information on who did the action is already in the ending. You don't need to say "Yo canto" (I sing), but just "Canto."

APPENDIX C. PRESENT TENSE

Examples of use of the present tense:

I sing, you sing, he sings, we sing, you guys sing, they sing
Canto, cantas, canta, cantamos, cantáis, cantan

I drink, you drink, he drinks, we drink, you guys drink, they drink
Bebo, bebes, bebe, bebemos, bebéis, beben

I live, you live, he lives, we live, you guys live, they live
Vivo, vives, vive, vivimos, vivís, viven

Unlike English, in Spanish you can use the present tense to describe historical facts.

Columbus discovered America in 1492.
Colón descubre America en 1492.

Spelling-changing or False-irregular Verbs

It may happen that the verb needs to alter its spelling to accommodate the right pronunciation. An example is **vencer** (= to defeat). If we add the endings to form the present tense, we obtain a wrong pronunciation of its forms. Venc-er /benthér/ → it should sound /benth-o/, but ~~venco~~ gives /benko/ instead.

	vencer
(I)	venzo
(you singular)	vences
(he/she/it)	vence
(we)	vencemos
(you guys)	vencéis
(they)	vencen

If you take the stem venc- and then add the suffix -o, the result is venco, but the "c" with "o" doesn't sound as "s" of vencer. That's why the spelling needs to change.

This happens with the verbs ending in:

```
-cer  → -zo
-cir  → -zo
-ger  → -jo
-gir  → -jo
-guir → -go
-quir → -co
```

Warning

> You don't have to memorize these endings. As you learn the rules of spelling of this book, you will notice when you write them (remember: pronunciation wise, they are regular). Notice that it is the same tranformation of:
> poco (= little of) + ito → poquito (= little bit of), not pocito

Examples:

	-cer → -zo	-cir → -zo	-ger → -jo
	vencer	esparcir	proteger
	= to defeat	= to spread	= to protect
(I)	venzo	esparzo	protejo
(you singular)	vences	esparces	proteges
(he/she/it)	vence	esparce	protege
(we)	vencemos	esparcimos	protegemos
(you guys)-Sp.	vencéis	esparcís	protegéis
(you guys/ they)	vencen	esparcen	protegen

	-gir → jo	-guir → -go	quie → -co
	exigir	distinguir	delinquir
	= to demand	= to distinguish	= to commit a crime
(I)	exijo	distingo	delinco
(you singular)	exiges	distingues	delinques
(he/she/it)	exige	distingue	delinque
(we)	exigimos	distinguimos	delinquimos
(you guys)-Sp.	exigís	distinguís	delinquís
(you guys/ they)	exigen	distinguen	delinquen

APPENDIX C. PRESENT TENSE

All these verbs are the spelling-changing verbs. Those that happen to be regular can also be called false-irregular verbs.

Also notice that these alterations can also happen when the verb is irregular for other reasons. For example "seguir" (= to follow) is truly irregular (not what we called "false irregular"). As it is explained in the following Corollary, Type 4, with the verb "seguir" forms "sigo" (I follow). So, it changes its stem; it is irregular. It is in addition to that, that it needs to alter its "u" to accommodate to the right pronunciation, according to the above rules ("sigo," not ~~siguo~~).

These alterations only take place with the Present tense, Preterite (*Chapter 23 Preterite)* and Present Subjunctive (*Chapter 28 Present Subjunctive*).

The Irregular Verbs in the Present Tense

There are six types of irregularities:

Type 1 Affects all verbs ending in –uir

These verbs add "**y**" after the stem to form present tense, except for the forms nosotros and vosotros.

Example: constru**ir** (= to construct) construo → constru**y**o

(I)	construyo
(you singular)	construyes
(he/she/it)	construye
(we)	construimos
(you guys) -Spain	construís
(you guys/ they)	construyen

Shading indicates irregularity

The rule of the slipper. Some Californian teachers use the term "la regla de la zapatilla" based on the shape that results when you display the conjugation in two columns:

construyo	construimos
construyes	construís
construye	construyen

Other examples are: atribuir, contribuir, distribuir (= to attribute, to contribute, to distribute).

Type 2. Affects most verbs with an -o- in the second to last syllable.

These verbs change -o- → -ue- , except for the forms nosotros and vosotros, to form present tense.

Example: dor-mir (= to sleep)

(I)	duermo
(you singular)	duermes
(he/she/it)	duerme
(we)	dormimos
(you guys) –Spain-	dormís
(you guys/ they)	duermen

Shading indicates irregularity

Notice the "rule of the slipper" explained above.

Other examples are: poder, morir, mover, contar (= can, to die, to move, to count).

Nonetheless, there are verbs like "co-mer," or "co-ser" (= to eat, to sew) which are regular.

Type 3. Affects most verbs with an –e- in the second to last syllable.

Some of these verbs change –e- → -ie- , except for the forms nosotros and vosotros. **Other verbs** of this type change according to the **type 4**.

Example: pre-fe-rir (= to prefer)

APPENDIX C. PRESENT TENSE

(I)	prefiero
(you singular)	prefieres
(he/she/it)	prefiere
(we)	preferimos
(you guys) –Spain-	preferís
(you guys/ they)	prefieren

Shading indicates irregularity

Notice that we have here the "rule of the slipper" explained above.

Other examples are: entender, querer, sentir (= to understand, to want, to feel).

Nonetheless, there are verbs like "be-ber" or "pesar" (= to drink, to weigh) which are regular.

Type 4. Affects most verbs with an –e- in the second to last syllable.

Some of these verbs change –e- → -i- , except for the forms nosotros and vosotros. Other verbs of this type change according to the previous type.

Example: re-pe-tir (= to repeat)

(I)	repito
(you singular)	repites
(he/she/it)	repite
(we)	repetimos
(you guys) –Spain-	repetís
(you guys/ they)	repiten

Shading indicates irregularity

Notice that we have here the "rule of the slipper" explained above.

Other examples are: seguir, conseguir, pedir (= to follow, to achieve, to ask for).

So, a verb with an –e- in the second to last syllable can be irregular ie-irregular i-irregular or regular (preferir, repetir, pensar).

Nonetheless, notice that, as in the previous type, there are verbs like "be-ber" or "pesar" (= to drink, to weigh) which are regular.

Type 5. Affects most verbs ending with –cer or –cir, except "decir."

These verbs add "z" before the "c," for the form "I." Example: producir (= to produce)

(I)	produzco
(you singular)	produces
(he/she/it)	produce
(we)	producimos
(you guys) –Spain-	producís
(you guys/ they)	producen

Shading indicates irregularity

Other examples are: conocer, conducir, crecer, (= to know, to drive, to grow up).

Nonetheless, there are verbs as "vencer" or "convencer" (= to defeat, to convince) which are regular.

Type 6. Others.

There are **21 verbs** which don't follow any rule. However they can be grouped by their similar changes.

12 verbs end with "–go" for the form of "I" (instead of "-o"). These are:

APPENDIX C. PRESENT TENSE

tener, venir, decir, bendecir, hacer, satisfacer, valer, traer, poner, salir, caer, oír.
(to have, to come, to say, to bless, to do, to satisfy, to be worth, to bring, to put, to go out, to fall, to hear)

	tener	**venir**
(I)	tengo	vengo
(you singular)	tienes	vienes
(he/she/it)	tiene	viene
(we)	tenemos	venimos
(you guys) –Spain-	tenéis	venís
(you guys/ they)	tienen	vienen

	decir	**bendecir ***
(I)	digo	bendigo
(you singular)	dices	bendices
(he/she/it)	dice	bendice
(we)	decimos	bendecimos
(you guys) –Spain-	decís	bendecís
(you guys/ they)	dicen	bendicen

	hacer	**satisfacer ***
(I)	hago	satisfago
(you singular)	haces	satisfaces
(he/she/it)	hace	satisface
(we)	hacemos	satisfacemos
(you guys) –Spain-	hacéis	satisfacéis
(you guys/ they)	hacen	satisfacen

	traer	**valer**	**poner**
(I)	traigo	valgo	pongo
(you singular)	traes	vales	pones
(he/she/it)	trae	vale	pone
(we)	traemos	valemos	ponemos
(you guys) –Spain-	traéis	valéis	ponéis
(you guys/ they)	traen	valen	ponen

Shading indicates irregularity

	salir	caer	oír
(I)	salgo	caigo	oigo
(you singular)	sales	caes	oyes
(he/she/it)	sale	cae	oye
(we)	salimos	caemos	oímos
(you guys) –Spain-	salís	caéis	oís
(you guys/ they)	salen	caen	oyen

(*) The rules are also applicable to all verbs that derive from them like "poner" and "suponer" (= to put and to suppose). However, although "satisfacer" and "bendecir" look like derivative verbs of hacer and decir respectively, they are not. You will see that they are not linked in other tenses.

Four verbs end with "–y" for the form of "I" (instead of "–o"). These are: dar, estar, ser, and ir (= to give, to be, to be, to go).

	dar	estar	ser	ir
(I)	doy	estoy	soy	voy
(you singular)	das	estás	eres	vas
(he/she/it)	da	está	es	va
(we)	damos	estamos	somos	vamos
(you guys) –Spain-	dais	estáis	sois	vais
(you guys/ they)	da	están	son	van

Five verbs don't have any specific ending. These are: saber, ver, caber, jugar, haber (= to know, to see, to fit, to play, to have –auxiliary).

	saber	ver	caber	jugar *	haber
(I)	sé	veo	quepo	juego	he
(you s.)	sabes	ves	cabes	juegas	has
(he/she/it)	sabe	ve	cabe	juega	ha
(we)	sabemos	vemos	cabemos	jugamos	hemos
(you guys) –Spain-	sabéis	veis	cabéis	jugáis	habéis
(you guys/ they)	saben	ven	caben	juegan	han

Shading indicates irregularity

(*) Notice that the verb "jugar" seems to fit into the type-2 irregularity (o → ue); however this verb does not have a "o," but an "u," in the second to last syllable.

Note about irregular verbs

Certain tenses share the same irregularities. You will see similar types of irregularities of the Present when you study the Present Subjunctive.

APPENDIX D

TABLE OF ENDINGS OF THE REGULAR VERBS
TABLA DE TERMINACIONES DE LOS VERBOS REGULARES

APPENDIX D: TABLE OF ENDINGS OF THE REGULAR VERBS
TABLA DE TERMINACIONES DE LOS VERBOS REGULARES

Impersonal Forms of the Verb

Infinitive (to sing)

AR verbs	ER verbs	IR verbs
-ar	-er	-ir

Gerund (singing)

AR verbs	ER verbs	IR verbs
-ando	-iendo	-iendo

Past Participle (sung)

AR verbs	ER verbs	IR verbs
-ado	-ido	-ido

Personal Forms of the Verb: Indicative Mood

Present (I sing)

	AR verbs	ER verbs	IR verbs
(I)	-o	-o	-o
(you singular)	-as	-es	-es
(he/she/it)	-a	-e	-e
(we)	-amos	-emos	-imos
(you guys) -Spain-	-ais	-éis	-ís
(you guys/ they)	-an	-en	-en

Preterite (I sang)

	AR verbs	ER verbs	IR verbs
(I)	-é	-í	-í
(you singular)	-aste	-iste	-iste
(he/she/it)	-ó	-ió	-ió
(we)	-amos	-imos	-imos
(you guys) -Spain-	-asteis	-isteis	-isteis
(you guys/ they)	-aron	-ieron	-ieron

Imperfect Past (I sang*)

	AR verbs	ER verbs	IR verbs
(I)	-aba	-ía	-ía
(you singular)	-abas	-ías	-ías
(he/she/it)	-aba	-ía	-ía
(we)	-ábamos	-íamos	-íamos
(you guys) -Spain-	-abais	-íais	-íais
(you guys/ they)	-aban	-ian	-ían

APPENDIX C. TABLE OF ENDINGS OF THE REGULAR VERBS 205

Future (I will sing)	AR verbs	ER verbs	IR verbs
(I)	-aré	-eré	-iré
(you singular)	-arás	-erás	-irás
(he/she/it)	-ará	-erá	-irá
(we)	-aremos	-eremos	-iremos
(you guys) -Spain-	-aréis	-eréis	-iréis
(you guys/ they)	-arán	-erán	-irán

Conditional (I would sing)	AR verbs	ER verbs	IR verbs
(I)	-aría	-ería	-iría
(you singular)	-arías	-erías	-irías
(he/she/it)	-aría	-ería	-iría
(we)	-aríamos	-eríamos	-iríamos
(you guys) -Spain-	-aríais	-eríais	-iríais
(you guys/ they)	-arían	-erían	-irían

Personal Forms of the Verb: Imperative Mood

Imperative (Sing!)	AR verbs	ER verbs	IR verbs
(I)			
(you singular)	-a	-e	-e
(he/she/it)			
(we)			
(you guys) -Spain-	-ad	-ed	-id
(you guys/ they)			

Personal Forms of the Verb: Subjunctive Mood

Present (...that I sing)	AR verbs	ER verbs	IR verbs
(I)	-e	-a	-a
(you singular)	-es	-as	-as
(he/she/it)	-e	-a	-a
(we)	-emos	-amos	-amos
(you guys) -Spain-	-éis	-áis	-áis
(you guys/ they)	-en	-an	-an

Past (...that I sang)	AR verbs	ER verbs	IR verbs
(I)	-ara	-iera	-iera
(you singular)	-aras	-ieras	-ieras
(he/she/it)	-ara	-iera	-iera
(we)	-áramos	-iéramos	-iéramos
(you guys) -Spain-	-arais	-ierais	-ierais
(you guys/ they)	-aran	-ieran	-ieran
-or-			
(I)	-ase	-iese	-iese
(you singular)	-ases	-ieses	-ieses
(he/she/it)	-ase	-iese	-iese
(we)	-ásemos	-iésemos	-iésemos
(you guys) -Spain-	-aseis	-ieseis	-ieseis
(you guys/ they)	-asen	-iesen	-iesen

INDEX OF GRAMMATICAL WORDS

INDEX OF GRAMMATICAL WORDS
ÍNDICE DE PALABRAS GRAMATICALES

The following is a list of words with grammatical meaning as explained in *Chapter 11 Grammar Rules*.

In the following table:

- Underscore indicates the point of stress. One vowel words or words with accent mark are not indicated.

- The ellipses (...) at the end of a term indicates that the word must be followed by a noun or an adjective, i.e. "any..." in "any patient can do it" vs "any" in "any can do it." The ellipses between two words indicates there is some content in between, e.g. "either or".

- A capitalized initial indicates the word or expression can function as a complete sentence, e.g. Hello.

- The last column gives a reference of the chapter where that word or that type of words are explained.

- Notice that no indication about the gender (masculine/ feminine) is needed: none of these words are nouns (nouns are not grammatical words)

INDEX OF GRAMMATICAL WORDS

#	English	Spanish	Chapter
1	a	un , una	6
2	a lot	mucho	6
3	a lot of…	mucho/a/os/as	6
4	according to	según	10
5	after	tras	10
6	against	contra	10
7	all	todo/a/os/as el/la/los/las…	6
8	although	aunque	10
9	and	y	10
10	another	otro/ a	6
11	any, whichever	cualquiera	6
12	any…, whichever	cualquier…	6
13	around…	alrededor de…	10
14	as	a medida que	10
15	as	como	10
16	as per	en cuanto a…	10
17	as soon as	tan pronto como	10
18	at	en, a	10
19	at/ in the beginning of…	al principio de…	10
20	at/ in the end of…	al final de	10
21	because	porque	10
22	because of	por	10
23	because of	por causa de	10
24	between, among	entre	10
25	both	los dos	6
26	but	pero	10
27	but	sino	10
28	by	por	10
29	due to	debido a	10
30	either…or…	o…o..	10
31	everything	todo	6
32	excuse me	Con permiso	4
33	far from	lejos de	10
34	for	para, por	10
35	from	desde, de	10
36	given that	dado que	10

#	English	Spanish	Chapter
37	Good afternoon	Buenas tardes	4
38	Good evening, night	Buenas noches	4
39	Good morning	Buenos días	4
40	Goodbye	Adiós	4
41	he	él	7
42	Hello	Hola	4
43	Help me!	¡Ayuda!	4
44	Help me!	¡Socorro!	4
45	her	su / sus	6
46	here	aquí, acá	5
47	hers	suyo /a / os / as	11
48	his (as in "his house")	su / sus	6
49	his (as in "This is his")	suyo /a / os / as	11
50	how (quest. & exclam.)	cómo	12
51	How long ago…?	¿Cuánto tiempo hace…?	12
52	How long…?	¿Por cuánto tiempo…?	12
53	How many…?	¿Cuánto/a/os/as…?	12
54	How much…?	¿Cuánto/a…?	12
55	How often…?	¿Con qué frecuencia…?	12
56	However	sin embargo	10
57	I	yo	7
58	I don't know.	No lo sé, No sé.	4
59	I wish!	Ojalá	4
60	I'm sorry	Perdón, Lo siento.	4
61	if	si	10
62	in	en	10
63	in case that	en el caso de que	10
64	in other words	en otras palabras	10
65	in spite of	a pesar de	10
66	in the middle of…	en medio de…	10
67	in view that	en vista de que, visto que	10
68	inside…	dentro de…	10
69	it	ello (to be omitted)	7
70	Its	su/ sus	6
71	Its	suyo /a / os / as	11
72	like	al igual que	10

#	English	Spanish	Chapter
73	like	como	10
74	little (amount)	poco	6
75	little (amount)...	poco/a ...	6
76	Maybe	Tal vez, Quizá(s)	4
77	Me neither	Yo tampoco	4
78	Me too	Yo también	4
79	me	me, mí	11
80	mine	mío/ a/ os/ as	11
81	much	mucho / mucha	6
82	much	muchos/as	6
83	my	mi / mis	6
84	near, close to, around...	cerca de...	10
85	neither ...nor...	ni...ni...	10
86	never	nunca , jamás	12
87	nevertheless	no obstante	10
88	next to...	junto a...	10
89	no	no	12
90	no...	ningún /ninguna	6
91	noe	ninguno / ninguna	6
92	none of...	ninguno/a de ...	6
93	not	no	12
94	nothing	nada	6
95	now	ahora	5
96	of the	del = de el	6
97	of you guys	su, vuestro/a/os/as (Sp.)	7
98	of, from, off	de	10
99	Okay	Okey	4
100	on	sobre, en	10
101	on top of...	encima de...	10
102	or	o	10
103	other, others	otro/ a/ os /as	6
104	our, ours	nuestro/ a / os/ as	7
105	outside...	fuera de...	10
106	Please	Por favor	4
107	Really?	¿De verdad?	4
108	Right?	¿Verdad?	4

#	English	Spanish	Chapter
109	See you later	Hasta la vista	4
110	See you later	Hasta luego	4
111	See you soon	Hasta pronto	4
112	she	ella	7
113	side by side...	al lado de	10
114	snce	puesto que, ya que	10
115	so that	para que	10
116	some	alguno /alguna	6
117	some of ...	alguno/a/os/as de...	6
118	some...	algún /a /os/ as, unos, unas	6
119	something	algo	6
120	supposing that	suponiendo que	10
121	Thank you	Gracias	4
122	Thank you very much	Muchas Gracias	4
123	that	aquel, aquella, aquello	6
124	that	ese/a, eso	6
125	the	el, la, los, las	6
126	their	su / sus	6
127	theirs	suyo /a / os / as	11
128	then, afterwards	entonces, luego	10
129	there	ahí, allí, allá	5
130	these	éstos/as	6
131	they	ellos	7
132	this	este/a, esto	6
133	those	ésos/as	6
134	those (farther)	aquellos/as	6
135	to	para, a	10
136	to herself	le, la, se	11
137	to herself	se	11
138	to him	le, lo, se	11
139	to himself	se	11
140	to it	le, la, lo, se	11
141	to itself	se	11
142	to me, to myself	me	11
143	to the, at the	al = a el	6
144	to themselves	se	11

INDEX OF GRAMMATICAL WORDS

#	English	Spanish	Chapter
145	to us, to ourselves	nos	11
146	to you (plural)	les, se	11
147	to you (s.), to yourself	te	11
148	to you guys, yourselves	os (Spain)	11
149	to, at	a	10
150	to, towards	hacia	10
151	today	hoy	5
152	tomorrow	mañana	5
153	under...	bajo...	10
154	underneath	debajo de / abajo de	10
155	unless	a menos que	10
156	until, up to	hasta	10
157	we	nosotros	7
158	what (in other cases)	que	12
159	what (quest. & exclam.)	qué	12
160	when	cuando, cuándo	12
161	where	donde, dónde	12
162	which (in other cases)	cual/cuales, cuál/cuáles	12
164	while, as long as	mientras	10
165	who	quien/quienes, quién/quiénes	12
166	with	con	10
167	with me	conmigo	11
168	with you (s.) informal	contigo	11
169	without	sin	10
171	yes	sí	12
172	yesterday	ayer	5
173	you (obj. pronoun)	te, ti	11
174	you (singular)	tú	7
175	you guys	ustedes	7
176	you guys	vosotros (Spain)	7
177	You're welcome	De nada	4
178	your	su / sus (informal)	6
179	your	tu / tus (singular)	6
180	yours	suyo /a /os /as (de usted)	11
181	yours	tuyo/ a / os /as (de ti)	11

INDEX OF TECHNICAL WORDS

INDEX OF TECHNICAL WORDS
ÍNDICE DE PALABRAS TÉCNICAS

The following is a list of the words from the Medical Vocabulary sections of this book

In the following table:

- Underscore indicates the point of stress. One vowel words or words with accent mark are not indicated.

- The last column gives a reference of the chapter where that word is used.

- All words are nouns with the exception of those of chapter 17, which include some adjectives. The gender of the nouns (masculine/ feminine) are indicated only if the word doesn't end in "o" or "a."

INDEX OF TECHNICAL WORDS 217

English	Spanish	Chapter
abdomen	(el) abdomen	6
abrasion	rozadura, raspadura	11
accident	(el) accidente	16
acid	ácido	10
acupressure	(la) acupresión, digitopuntura	15
acupuncture	acupuntura	15
addiction	(la) adicción	13
AIDS	(el) SIDA	13
air	(el) aire	10
alcoholism	alcoholismo	13
allergy	alergia	13
Alzheimer	(el) Alzheimer	13
ambulance	(el) ambulancia	17
amnesia	amnesia	13
amniotic liquid	líquido amniótico	9
amp	amperio	16
amputation	(la) amputación	15
analysis	(el) análisis	12
anesthesia	anestesia	14
anesthesiologist	(el/ la) anestesista	4
anesthesiology	anestesiología	3
ankle	tobillo	6
anorexia	anorexia	13
antacid	antiácido	14
anti depressive	antidepresivo	14
antibiotic	antibiótico	14
anticoagulant	(el) anticoagulante	14
antidote	antídoto	14
antihistaminic	antihistamínico	14
anus	ano	7
anxiety	(la) ansiedad	11
appendix	(el) apéndice	7
appointment	cita	17
arm	brazo	6
armpit	axila	6
arterial	arterial	17
artery	arteria	9
arthritis	(la) artritis	13

English	Spanish	Chapter
artificial leg, arm	(la) pierna, brazo artificial	17
asphyxia	asfixia	11
aspirin	aspirina	14
asthma	(el) asma	13
astigmatism	astigmatismo	13
atrophy	atrofia	13
avian flu	(la) gripe aviar	13
baby	(el) bebé	17
back	espalda	6
bacteria	bacteria	13
bacterial	bacteriano	17
bandage	venda	14
band-aid	curita, tirita	14
base	(la) base	10
bile	(la) bilis	9
biopsy	biopsia	12
bite (from dog, etc.)	mordedura	11
bite (from mosquito, etc)	picadura	11
bladder	vejiga	7
blister	ampolla	11
blood	(la) sangre	9
blood (blood related)	sanguíneo	17
blood test	(el) análisis de sangre	12
blood transfusion	(la) transfusión de sangre	15
blood vessel	vaso sanguíneo	9
body	cuerpo	6
bone	hueso	9
bones	huesos	8
bottom	trasero	6
brain	cerebro	7
bronchi	bronquio	7
bronchial	bronquial	17
bronchitis	(la) bronquitis	13
bruise	(el) moratón, (el) hematoma	11
bucal	bucal	17
bump	(el) chichón	11
burn	quemadura	11
calcium	calcio	10

INDEX OF TECHNICAL WORDS 219

English	Spanish	Chapter
calf	pantorrilla	6
cancer	(el) cáncer	13
capillary	(el) capilar	9
capsule	cápsula	14
car accident	(el) accidente de carro	16
carbohydrate	carbohidrato	10
cardiac	cardíaco	17
cardiac arrest	paro cardiaco	16
cardiologist	cardiólogo/ a	4
cardiology	cardiología	3
carpus	carpo	8
cartilage	cartílago	9
cast	escayola	17
cataracts	(las) cataratas	13
catheter, probe	(el) catéter, sonda	12
cell	célula	17
cerebral	cerebral	17
cheek	carrillo	5
chemical	producto químico	10
chemotherapy	quimioterapia	15
chest	pecho	6
chickenpox	varicela	13
chin	barbilla	5
chlorine	cloro	10
chocking	atragantamiento	17
choking	atragantamiento	16
circulatory system	aparato circulatorio	2
circumcision	(la) circuncisión	15
cirrhosis	(la) cirrosis	13
clavicle	clavícula	8
clot	coágulo	13
CO	monóxido de carbono	10
CO2	dióxido de carbono	10
cold	resfriado, constipado	13
colon	(el) colon	7
condom	(el) condón, preservativo	14
congestion	(la) congestión	11
constipation	estreñimiento	11

English	Spanish	Chapter
contraceptive pill	píldora anticonceptiva	14
contraction	(la) contracción	11
cotton ball	(el) algodón	12
cough	(la) tos	11
cough syrup	(el) jarabe para la tos	14
CPR	(la) RCP *	15
cramp	(el) calambre	11
cream	crema	14
crutches	(las) muletas	17
CT scan	(el) TAC *	12
cubic centimeter	centímetro cúbico	16
cut	(el) corte	11
degree (of temperature)	grado (de temperatura)	16
delivery	parto	17
dementia	demencia	13
dental	dental	17
dentist	(el, la) dentista	4
dentistry	odontología	3
depression	(la) depresión	13
dermatologist	dermatólogo/ a	4
dermatology	dermatología	3
diabetes	(la) diabetes	13
diagnostics	(el) diagnóstico	12
dialysis	(la) diálisis	15
diaphragm	(el) diafragma	7
diarrhea	diarrea	11
digestive system	aparato digestivo	2
diphtheria	difteria	13
disease	(la) enfermedad	13
disorder	(el) desorden	13
DNA	(el) ADN (a-de-ene)	17
doctor, physician	doctor/ a, (el/ la) médico	4
Down syndrome	(el) síndrome de Down	13
dressing	vendado	15
drug	medicamento	14
drug addiction	(la) drogadicción	13
ear	oreja	5
earwax	(el) cerumen	9

INDEX OF TECHNICAL WORDS

English	Spanish	Chapter
echocardiogram	(el) ecocardiograma	12
elbow	codo	6
element	elemento	10
embryo	(el) embrión	17
endocrine system	aparato endocrino	2
endoscopy	endoscopia	12
ENT (ear, nose and throat)	otorrinolaringología	3
ENT specialist	otorrino/ otorrinolaringólogo/a	4
epidural	(la) epidural	14
esophagus	esófago	7
excretory system	aparato excretor	2
explosion	(la) explosión	16
eye	ojo	5
eye drop	colirio	12
eyebrow	ceja	5
eyelash	pestaña	5
eyelid	párpado	5
face	cara	5
falange	(la) falange	8
fall	caída	16
fat	grasa	10
feces, poop	(las) heces, caca	9
feet	(el) pie	16
femur	(el) fémur	8
fetus	feto	17
fever	(la) fiebre	11
fibula	(el) peroné	8
fight	pelea	16
finger	dedo	6
fire	incendio	16
fireman	bombero	17
flea	pulga	13
flu	(la) gripe	13
fluid	fluido	9
fluoride	fluoruro	10
fluorine	(el) flúor	10
foot	(el) pie	6
forearm	antebrazo	6

English	Spanish	Chapter
forehead	(la) frente	5
fracture	fractura	13
fungi	(los) hongos	13
gallbladder	vesícula	7
gallon	galón	16
gas	(el) gas	10
gastric acid	jugo gástrico	9
gastroenterologist	gastroenterólogo/ a	4
gastroenterology	gastroenterología	3
gel	(el) gel	14
genitals	(los) genitales	6
geriatrics	geriatría	3
gerontologist	(el, la) geriatra	4
gland	glándula	9
gloves	(el) guante	12
glucose	glucosa	10
glycerine	glicerina	10
gonorrhea	gonorrea	13
gram/ milligram/ kilogram	gramo/ miligramo/ kilogramo	16
groin	(la) ingle	6
gum	encía	5
gynecologist	ginecólogo/ a	4
gynecology	ginecología	3
hair	pelo	5
hair	pelo, cabello	6
hand	(la) mano	6
head	cabeza	5
head	cabeza	6
heart	(el) corazón	7
heart attack	(el) ataque al corazón	13
heart murmur	soplo	13
hepatic	hepático	17
hepatitis	(la) hepatitis	13
herpes	(los) herpes	13
hip	cadera	6
hip	cadera	8
HIV	(el) VIH *	13
hormone	hormona	9

English	Spanish	Chapter
humerus	húmero	8
hydration	(la) hidratación	15
hydrogen	hidrógeno	10
ice	hielo	10
immunity	(la) inmunidad	17
inch	pulgada	16
incident	(el) incidente	16
infant	(el) lactante	17
infection	(la) infección	17
inflammation	(la) inflamación	11
inner ear	oído	5
insomnia	insomnio	13
integumentary system	aparato integumentario	2
internal medicine	medicina interna	3
intestinal	intestinal	17
intestine	intestino	7
intubation	sonda	14
investigation	(la) investigación	17
iodine	yodo	10
iron	hierro	10
irritation	(la) irritación	11
itching	(la) picazón	11
IV, saline	suero, suero fisiológico	14
kidney	(el) riñón	7
kinesiologist	kinesiólogo/ a	4
kinesiology	kinesiología, quinesiología	3
knee	rodilla	6
large intestine	intestino grueso	7
larynx	(la) laringe	7
leg	pierna	6
ligament	ligamento	9
lip	labio	5
liquid	líquido	10
liter/ milliliter	mililitro	16
liver	hígado	7
lotion	(la) loción	14
louse	piojo	13
lump	bulto	11

English	Spanish	Chapter
lung	(el) pulmón	7
lymphatic	linfático	17
lymphatic node	nódulo linfático	9
lymphatic system	aparato linfático	2
lymphatic vessel	vaso linfático	9
mammary gland	glándula mamaria	9
mammogram	mamografía	12
mandible	mandíbula	8
mandible	mandíbula	5
mask	mascarilla	12
massage	(el) masaje	15
medical	médico	17
medical specialties	(las) especialidades médicas	3
medication	(la) medicación	15
medicine	medicina	3
meningitis	(la) meningitis	13
menstrual pain	(el) dolor menstrual	11
mercury	mercurio	10
metacarpus	metacarpo	8
metal	(el) metal	10
metatarsus	metatarso	8
meter/ mm/ cm	metro/ milímetro, centímetro	16
microscope	microscopio	12
midwife	comadrona	4
migraine	migraña	13
millimeter of mercury	milímetro de mercurio	16
mineral	(el) mineral	10
monitor	(el) monitor	12
mouth	boca	5
MRI	(el) IRM **, tomografía	12
mucosa	mucosa	9
mucus, snot	moco	9
mumps	(las) paperas	13
muscle	músculo	9
muscular	muscular	17
musculoskeletal system	aparato locomotor	2
myopia	miopía	13
nail	uña	6

INDEX OF TECHNICAL WORDS

English	Spanish	Chapter
nasal	nasal	17
nausea, dizziness	náusea, mareo	11
navel	ombligo	6
neck	nuca, cuello	5
needle	aguja	12
nerve	nervio	9
nervous systems	aparato nervioso	2
neurologist	neurólogo/ a	4
neurology	neurología	3
newborn	(el) recién nacido	17
nipple	(el) pezón	6
nitrogen	nitrógeno	10
nose	(la) nariz	5
nurse	enfermero/ a	4
nursing	enfermería	3
nutrient	(el) nutriente	10
obesity	(la) obesidad	13
obstetrics	obstetricia	3
ocular	ocular	17
ointment	pomada	14
oncologist	oncólogo/ a	4
oncology	oncología	3
ophthalmologist	oftalmólogo/ a, (el/ la) oculista	4
ophthalmology	oftalmología	3
organ	órgano	7
osteoporosis	(la) osteoporosis	13
otitis	(la) otitis	13
ounce	onza	16
ovary	ovario	7
overdose	(la) sobredosis	16
oxygen	oxígeno	10
oxygen mask	mascarilla de oxígeno	14
oxytocin, pitosin	oxitocina	14
pace maker	(el) marcapasos	17
pain, ache	(el) dolor	11
palate	(el) paladar	5
palpitations	(las) palpitaciones	11
pancreas	(el) páncreas	7

English	Spanish	Chapter
pancreatic	pancreático	17
paralysis	(la) parálisis	13
paramedic	paramédico/ a	4
Parkinson	(el) Parkinson	13
paste	pasta	14
patella	rótula	8
patient	(el) paciente	17
pediatrician	(el, la) pediatra	4
pediatrics	pediatría	3
pediatrics	pediatría	3
pelvis	(la) pelvis	8
penis	(el) pene	7
peritonitis	(la) peritonitis	13
pharmacist	farmacéutico/ a	4
pharmacy	farmacia	3
pharyngitis	(la) faringitis	13
pharynx	(la) faringe	7
phlebitis	(la) flebitis	13
phlegm	flema	9
physical therapist	(el/la) fisioterapeuta	4
physical therapy	fisioterapia	3
physiotherapy	fisioterapia	15
pill	píldora, pastilla,	14
pimple	grano	11
placenta	placenta	7
pneumonia	neumonía	13
poison	veneno	17
policeman	(el) policía	17
potassium	potasio	10
pound	libra	16
powder	(los) polvos	14
practitioner	(el/ la) médico de familia	4
prescription	receta médica	17
prevention	(la) prevención	17
procedure	procedimiento	12
prognosis	(la) evolución esperada	17
prostate	próstata	7
prostatic	prostático	17

INDEX OF TECHNICAL WORDS

English	Spanish	Chapter
protein	proteína	10
psychiatric	psiquiátrico	17
psychiatrist	(el, la) psiquiatra	4
psychiatry	psiquiatría	3
psychologist	psicólogo/ a	4
psychology	psicología	3
psychotherapy	psicoterapia	15
pubis	(el) pubis	6
pulmonary	pulmonar	17
pulmonologist	neumólogo/ a	4
pulmonology	neumología	3
pupil	pupila	5
radiographer	radiólogo/ a	4
radiology	radiología	3
radiotherapy	radioterapia	15
radius	radio	8
rectal	rectal	17
rectum	recto	7
referral	(el) volante	17
reflux	reflujo	13
rehabilitation	(la) rehabilitación	15
reimplantation	(la) reimplante	15
renal	renal	17
reproductive system	aparato reproductor	2
respiratory arrest	paro respiratorio	16
respiratory system	aparato respiratorio	2
result	resultado	17
resuscitation	(la) reanimación	15
rheumatism	reumatismo	13
rib	costilla	8
RICE	descanso, hielo, compresión, el.	15
ruler	regla	12
runny nose	moqueo	11
saliva	saliva	9
salt	(la) sal	10
sample	muestra	12
scalpel	escalpelo, (el) bisturí	12
scapula	omóplato	8

English	Spanish	Chapter
scissors	(las) tijeras	12
scoliosis	(la) escoliosis	13
semen	(el) semen	9
serum	suero	14
shingles	(los) herpes zóster	13
shooting	tiroteo	16
shoulder	hombro	6
skin	(la) piel	9
skin graft	injerto de piel	15
skull	cráneo	8
sleep	sueño	11
small intestine	intestino delgado	7
sneeze	estornudo	11
social work	trabajo social	3
social worker	trabajador/a social	4
sodium	sodio	10
sole	planta	6
solid	sólido	10
specialist	(el, la) especialista	4
specialists	especialistas	4
sphincter	(el) esfínter	7
spinal cord	espina dorsal	7
spine	(la) columna vertebral	8
spleen	bazo	7
square centimeter	centímetro cuadrado	16
stabbing	puñalada	16
statistics	estadística	17
STD	(la) enf. de trasmisión sexual	13
sternum	(el) esternón	8
stethoscope	estetoscopio	12
sting	picadura	11
stomach	estómago	7
strangulation	(la) estrangulación	16
stress, anxiety	(el) estrés, (la) ansiedad	13
stroke	(el) ataque cerebral	13
stroke	(el) derrame cerebral	16
sulphur	(el) azufre	10
sunburn	quemadura solar	11

INDEX OF TECHNICAL WORDS

English	Spanish	Chapter
surgeon	cirujano/ a	4
surgery	cirugía	3
surgery	cirugía	15
suture	sutura	12
suture	sutura	15
sweat	(el) sudor	9
swelling	(la) hinchazón	11
symptom	(el) síntoma	11
syphilis	(la) sífilis	13
syringe	jeringuilla	12
syringe	jeringuilla	14
syrup	(el) jarabe	14
tablet	tableta, pastilla	14
tarsus	tarso	8
tattoo	(el) tatuaje	17
tear	lágrima	9
technician	(el, la) técnico	4
temple	(la) sien	5
tendons	(el) tendón	9
test	prueba, (el) test	12
testicle	testículo	7
tetanus	(el) tétanos	13
therapist	(el, la) terapeuta	4
therapy	terapia	3
therapy	terapia	15
thermometer	termómetro	12
thigh	muslo	6
throat	garganta	5
thrombosis	(la) trombosis	13
thyroid	(la) tiroides	9
tibia	tibia	8
tissue	tejido	9
toe	dedo	6
tongue	lengua	5
tool	herramienta	12
tooth	(el) diente	5
tourniquet	(el) torniquete	15
toxin	toxina	17

English	Spanish	Chapter
trachea	tráquea	7
transplant	(el) transplante	15
traumatologist	traumatólogo/ a	4
traumatology	traumatología	3
treatment and prevention	tratamiento y prevención	14
treatment procedure	procedimiento de tratamiento	15
tuberculosis	(la) tuberculosis	13
tumor	(el) tumor	13
typhus	(el) tifus	13
ulna	cúbito	8
ultrasonography	ultrasonido, ecografía	12
unit	(la) unidad	16
unusual tiredness	fatiga, cansancio	11
ureters	(el) uréter	9
urethra	uretra	9
urine analysis	(el) análisis de orina	12
urine, piss	orina, (el) pis	9
urologist	urólogo/ a	4
urology	urología	3
uterus	útero	7
vaccine	vacuna	14
vagina	vagina	7
vaginal	vaginal	17
varicose veins	(las) varices	13
vas deferens	vaso deferente	9
vasectomy	vasectomía	15
vein	vena	9
venereal disease	(la) enfermedad venérea	13
venom	veneno	17
venous	venoso	17
vertebra	vértebra	8
vessel	vaso	9
viral	viral	17
virus	(el) virus	13
visitor	visita	17
vitamin A, B, etc.	vitamina A, B, etc.	10
volt	voltio	16
vomiting	vómito	11

INDEX OF TECHNICAL WORDS

English	Spanish	Chapter
wart	verr<u>u</u>ga	13
water	(el) <u>a</u>gua	10
water steam	(el) vap<u>o</u>r de <u>a</u>gua	10
weight scale	p<u>e</u>so, bal<u>a</u>nza	12
wheel chair	s<u>i</u>lla de ru<u>e</u>das	17
whooping cough	(la) tos fer<u>i</u>na	13
wrist	muñ<u>e</u>ca	6
X ray	(los) r<u>a</u>yos X (<u>e</u>kis)	12

USING ENGLISH TO LEARN SPANISH
BOOKS OF THE SERIES

SPANISH FOR HEALTH CARE

Spanish for the Health Care is intended **for professionals** with no previous knowledge of Spanish. **The goal is to communicate with patients**. The book focuses on the dialogue to understand symptoms, and convey diagnostics and instructions.

> *The right way for professionals to learn Spanish is to learn the Spanish of the profession.*

SPANISH FOR ENGINEERS

Spanish for the Engineers is intended **for professionals** with no previous knowledge of Spanish. **The goal is to communicate in your technical environment**. Each chapter focuses on one specialty, including construction, software, M&E engineering and project managent.

> *The right way for professionals to learn Spanish is to learn the Spanish of the profession.*

SPANISH FOR CALIFORNIANS

Spanish for Californians shows the Spanish of **Latin America and the U.S.** One of the twenty-two Academies that represent Spanish is in the U.S. The book teaches the common within the norm.

> *A textbook for beginners, and a reference data book for speakers. The easiest way to learn is by learning the simplest first.*

ADVANCED SPANISH

Advanced Spanish focuses on **those topics that are an obstacle for your fluent Spanish**. The textbook explains the subjects with many examples and comparisons to English.

> *Now that you can communicate, it is time to get to the point and perfect your Spanish.*

www.ingramcontent.com/pod-product-compliance
Lightning Source LLC
Chambersburg PA
CBHW020755160426
43192CB00006B/336